WISE UP!

Thank you for supporting
Mainstg truth. al hope you
find part of this book useful.

Edward [signature]

WISE UP!

A PORTFOLIO MANAGER'S GUIDE TO BETTER INVESTMENT DECISIONS

Edward J. Silverstein

iUniverse, Inc.

New York Lincoln Shanghai

Wise Up!
A Portfolio Manager's Guide to Better Investment Decisions

Copyright © 2007 by Emaginesites LLC

iUniverse books may be ordered through booksellers or by contacting:

iUniverse
2021 Pine Lake Road, Suite 100
Lincoln, NE 68512
www.iuniverse.com
1-800-Authors (1-800-288-4677)

The views expressed in this work are solely those of the author and do not necessarily reflect the views of the publisher, and the publisher hereby disclaims any responsibility for them.

ISBN-13: 978-0-595-42751-2 (pbk)
ISBN-13: 978-0-595-68139-6 (cloth)
ISBN-13: 978-0-595-87081-3 (ebk)
ISBN-10: 0-595-42751-0 (pbk)
ISBN-10: 0-595-68139-5 (cloth)
ISBN-10: 0-595-87081-3 (ebk)

Printed in the United States of America

Contents

List of Tables

Preface

This book will make better investors of people who have a lot, a little or absolutely no experience in the stock market, but want to use their intelligence, common sense, and knowledge and curiosity about the world to make better and more profitable investment decisions. There is no simple formula for successful investing. Successful investing is part common sense, hard work, knowledge, and art form. Hopefully what follows will impart some of these qualities to those who read it.

Although I am a professional investor, I wrote this book in an easy to understand style. As my college professors can attest, I was a poor student of finance and accounting—I found the subjects extremely boring. Once in the working world, though, I discovered that finance was exciting and dynamic. However, having been through the drudgery of textbook and classroom learning, I wanted to write a book for others that would make finance and investing easy to understand, interesting, useful, and relevant.

This book will primarily address the skills and knowledge needed to successfully invest in publicly traded stocks, but some of the topics discussed will also aid the reader in evaluating investments in other asset types, such as real estate, private businesses, and fixed income instruments, such as bonds.

PART I

Where To Find Investment Ideas

Our goal of earning profits in the stock market is achieved by finding good businesses in which to invest. The business must be public, that is, it must have shares that trade on an exchange otherwise it will be difficult for the average person to participate as an investor in the business. *Idea Generation* is the process by which investors come up with potential companies to research and consider for investment.

The idea generation stage is probably the most random phase of the investment process. Ideas can come from many sources. Investors can find attractive investments through the ordinary course of their day. Many public companies make products that we encounter on a daily basis—Proctor & Gamble, Colgate, General Motors, Anheuser-Busch, etc. Some investors may find investment ideas through their occupation or profession. A doctor may learn of a promising new drug coming from a pharmaceutical company and may consider that company a good investment candidate. Building contractors may be familiar with construction equipment made by companies such as Caterpillar or Deere. With the abundance of financial news in the media, it is common to learn of investment ideas while watching the CNBC network or reading publications such as *The Wall Street Journal*, *Business Week*, or *Barrons*. All of these sources are good idea generators.

Before an investor begins to conduct in-depth research on an investment idea, he or she should ask if the company appears to be a good business. The investor may like the product or service that the company provides, but that does not necessarily mean that the company is a good business. A bar or restaurant that allows friends of the owner to run up large tabs may be a great place to hang out and eat, but it is unlikely to be a successful business. A successful business should offer a product or service that the public demands. The business should have high barriers to entry. Barriers to entry are what prevent imitators from copying a successful concept and taking some of that business for themselves. A successful business should have some characteristic that distinguishes it from its competitors. This can take the form of very low prices, a high level of service, or a product that cannot be found elsewhere. We also want to find a business that is well-managed, so that it can translate all of these positive attributes into a profitable enterprise.

Generally, we want to find businesses that are in stable and improving industries. What I mean by this is, we do not want to buy the best house in the worst neighborhood. A business may be well-run and better than its competitors, but if the industry in which they operate is in decline, even the best-run business is likely to struggle. A good example of this can be seen in the airline industry. Jet Blue and Southwest Airlines are arguably the two best-run airlines. They enjoy high levels of customer satisfaction. Both companies are led by excellent management teams that have done a very good job of running each airline. Unfortunately, however, the airline industry is plagued by long-term problems such as over-capacity, low barriers to entry, and high fuel prices. By over-capacity, we mean too much supply. There are too many airlines flying too many planes for companies to be able to earn healthy profits. When there are too many items (airline seats) for sale at any one time, the price tends to drop. The low barriers to entry in the airline industry virtually ensure that there will always be an oversupply of airline planes and seats. Contrary to what most people might think, it is actually very easy to start an airline. There is a surplus of used planes that can be acquired for little money. Lenders are eager to advance money to airline upstarts since they use the plane as collateral for the loan. Operating an airline is an exciting business and so there is never a shortage of entrepreneurs eager to try their luck. In addition, the airlines operate what is essentially a commodity business—transportation. With a commodity business, each company is producing or supplying essentially the same good or service. If the product provided is essentially the same, there is little brand loyalty, and consumers will base their purchase decision almost entirely on price. As a result, the companies that provide this product are constantly undercutting each other on price. It is very difficult for competitors to earn profits. With all these problems in the industry, it is easy to see why Southwest and Jetblue, despite their superior business plans, management, and execution, have been poor performing stocks. As investors, we want to find the best houses in the best neighborhoods; the best stocks in the best industries.

Lastly, what investors want to see, in addition to a solid business, is some future catalyst that will make the company more valuable and cause the stock price to rise. A catalyst can take many forms. Generally, a catalyst is something that the investor believes will occur in the future that will make the business more profitable and more attractive to investors. An example of a catalyst is the aging of the American population that will lead to increased demand for many goods and services such as leisure and travel services, medical care, or retirement housing. These businesses may be doing well now, but in the ensuing years, they should see their fortunes improve as a larger segment of the population seeks out these companies to provide them with the goods and services they require. A catalyst need not be so broad or far off. A catalyst can be the knowledge that a new product is being introduced by a company that will lead to a surge in sales. For example, technology savvy investors who believed that the iPod would be a huge selling item would have been wise to purchase shares of Apple Computer. Similarly, investors who rightly guessed that the increased demand for oil in China would send the price upward, were wise to buy shares of companies that drill for and produce petroleum. Just as early real estate speculators capitalized on their knowledge of where the highways would be built in order to scoop up land to resell to developers, so should stock investors look for the "coming of the highway" that will catapult a company's share price higher.

To summarize, a good investment will usually consist of a good business in a healthy industry, with some possible future catalyst that will make the company more desirable to other investors.

Finding Information

Where should investors look to find information on a particular company and its stock? Investors can conduct nearly all of their research from home using the Internet. A wealth of information can usually be found on a company's own web site. Most company web sites will include a description of the company and its operations. In addition, the site will often include recent Security and Exchange Commission (S.E.C.) filings of important annual and quarterly financial statements and disclosures. Much more valuable information can be obtained through general internet searches using websites such as Yahoo! and Google.

In addition to company specific information, it is advisable that investors read publications such as *The Wall Street Journal* and *Barrons* to keep abreast of market activity and business trends. However, it is important that investors not rely on these publications for investment advice. It is important that investors do their own research and not place too much credibility in the opinions of others who may have a self-interest in expressing certain opinions. Hedge fund managers will speak in glowing terms about stocks that they own. They are often motivated by a desire to get other investors to buy the stocks that they are touting, in an effort to get the share price higher so that they can then sell their holdings at a profit. I like to read other investors' opinions simply to generate new investment ideas for my own portfolio. However, I never invest without doing my own research and I rarely allow someone else's opinion to color my judgment.

Another source of investment information is the wealth of research reports written by analysts at brokerage firms such as Merrill Lynch, Smith Barney, and Goldman Sachs. There are several problems with relying too heavily on the opinions expressed in these reports. For one, these reports are proprietary and may not be easily obtained by investors who do not have accounts at the firms that publish them. That aside, it is important to remember that the analysts who write the reports are often wrong in their predictions about whether a particular stock will go up or down. In the past, many analysts have been overly optimistic in their predictions for the stocks that they research.

Many firms and their analysts have been accused of writing glowing reports on the companies that they research in an attempt to curry favor with the managements of these companies. By being on good terms with management, the brokerage firms hopes to win lucrative investment banking business from these companies. This conflict of interest made the headlines several years ago after the Internet stock bubble collapsed and investors sued various brokerage firms claiming that they relied on these bullish (positive) investment reports when making their investment decisions. The brokerage industry collectively paid billions of dollars to settle these suits and agreed to have future analyst reports more accurately reflect the analyst/author's true beliefs about a company's prospects.

My philosophy is that it can be useful to read these research reports and see why an analyst likes or dislikes a particular company's stock. I find them to be somewhat helpful but I never place too much emphasis on the author's opinion or price target for a given company. Relying on the opinions of others can sometimes prove costly. Hopefully after reading this book and learning from experience, you will be able to achieve superior results purely through your own efforts, without relying on the opinions of others.

If possible, investors should familiarize themselves with any company they are considering for their investment portfolio. At the very least, if the company has a website, give it a look. If the company is a retailer, visit several of the stores. Are they crowded? Are the employees helpful? Was the shopping experience positive—did you like the merchandise, prices, service, etc? If you like the store, chances are good that other consumers do as well. It is important not to generalize too much based on one or two visits, but it is important to physically see and experience what you are researching. Often, an investment that looks good on paper appears for different when viewed in person.

It is also important that investors understand what information to avoid when making investment decisions. Never respond to unsolicited emails, faxes, or mailings. Nearly all of these are sent out by scam artists trying to separate you from your money. It also is best to avoid unsolicited calls from stock brokers pitching individual stocks. It is not improper for brokers to call in an attempt to get you to open an account with their firm, but stay away from brokers who are from unknown firms who call pitching investment ideas. Many of these brokers are shady characters. Do not rely on advice offered at cocktail parties, tips from friends, relatives, barbers, or cab drivers. Rely on yourself. The purpose of this book is to enable you to conduct useful, fundamental research on almost any company.

THE 10-K

At this point, our discussion will take a more detailed and technical look at methods of investment analysis. Some of the concepts discussed may take several readings for the novice investor to grasp. If you find the following material tedious, or difficult to understand, please skip to Part II of this book and return to this section when you feel a bit braver. It is important that the reader eventually understand this material since it is the heart of investment analysis and essential for an in-depth evaluation of a company and its stock. I have attempted to write this section in an easy to understand style, so please don't be intimidated. I am hardly a genius. If I could get it to sink into my head, so can you.

Having discussed various sources of investment information, let's start our research process utilizing what I believe to be the most comprehensive and valuable source of information to the investor—a company's 10-K Form. The 10-K is a report that every public company must file annually with the S.E.C. (the Securities and Exchange Commission—the governmental body that enforces the securities laws in the United States). The 10-K contains a wealth of useful information for investors; information pertaining to the company's business operations, its executives, and its financial condition. The 10-K is usually the single best source of information for the investor evaluating a company for possible investment. Any company's 10K can be found at the SEC's web site: www.sec.gov.

How To Read And Use A 10-K

Understanding A Company's Balance Sheet, Income Statement, Statement Of Cash Flows, And Other Information Contained In A Company's Various S.E.C. Filings

Once an investor has established an interest in a company as a possible invest-ment, the first step toward analyzing its merits and risks involves a reading of the company's annual 10-K Form. The 10-K is a report that every publicly traded company must file with the SEC. The 10-K describes the business and provides a wealth of financial information, a listing of risk factors associated with the business, and other useful information about the management of the company and the industry in which the company operates. I will go through several 10-K filings to highlight what I look for, both positive attributes and potential pitfalls, when analyzing prospective investments.

Costco Wholesale Corp.

The first 10-K we will examine is Costco Wholesale Corporation (*ticker symbol COST*). Costco recently came to my attention after the company announced that profits for the coming quarter would be lower than most analysts' forecasts. The reason the company gave for the earnings shortfall was that the rising price of petroleum was hurting profits from its retail fuel sales. At first, this explana-tion made little sense to me. Were consumers buying less gasoline because prices were high? That seemed unlikely—usually car owners will drive no mat-ter what the cost of fuel. A call to the company's investor relations department cleared up the confusion. Apparently, Costco has a policy of always having the lowest retail price of gasoline in the areas in which they operate. On average, the company sells out its fuel tanks daily versus weekly for a traditional gas station, which sells far fewer gallons of gas per day. In a period of sharply rising fuel prices, Costco has to replenish its tanks at ever higher prices, whereas the tradi-tional retailer continues to sell gasoline purchased earlier in the week at lower prices. If Costco sticks to its policy of always having the lowest price for gaso-line, it will be forced to sell gasoline at, or sometimes even below, cost. This hurts profits. Once this was explained to me, the earnings shortfall made sense. It also did not seem to be something that would hurt the business for long, and might even be a positive if the price of fuel were to fall.

Most consumers know Costco as the warehouse-style retailer of food, with its large "warehouse—size" food packages, and other consumer products. Many investors who have shopped in the company's stores might believe that the company is a good investment. The stores are usually crowded and generally the company's word of mouth reputation is positive.

As investors, however, we don't just want to know, "Is this a good place to shop?", but, instead, "Is this a good business in which to invest?" Let's start with Costco's 2004 10-K and take a look. (Costco's 2004 10K—filing can be found at: http://www.sec.gov/Archives/edgar/data/909832/000119312504195535/d10k. htm) Costco's 10-K is fairly straightforward. The first section in Part I describes Costco's business and gives a brief history of the company. Your reading of this section should give you a basic understanding of the company's operations. It should also help you think of questions whose answers would be useful in determining whether this is a stock that we might want to purchase. For example, in the Business Description section of the 10-K, the company states that Costco offers members, "very low prices on a limited selection of nationally branded and selected private label products." It would be helpful to know how much lower are Costco's prices versus a traditional retail store. Also, how limited is the selection? Are the prices low enough to draw in shoppers without turning them off with too limited a selection? Perhaps the best way to answer this question would be to visit a store.

Reading further on in the "Business" section we see that Costco's warehouse stores carry approximately 4,000 SKU's (stock-keeping units) versus traditional supermarkets that traditionally carry 40-60,000 SKU's. Based on this statement it should be clear that Costco offers a very different shopping experience versus a traditional supermarket. As investors, we need to ask ourselves whether the lower prices at Costco are a big enough plus for shoppers, to offset the inconvenience of the more limited store hours, the much more limited selection, and the fact that shoppers have to purchase a membership card in order to purchase items in the store. If the answer to these questions is no, that shoppers will not tolerate these inconveniences, then Costco will probably not be a very good investment. If the answer is yes, it leads us to more questions— are the prices so low, that, yes, they can attract many shoppers but are too low for the company to earn a decent return on its investment in stores and merchandise? To answer this question, and others, we will need to look at the financial statements that appear further on in the 10-K. We will do that shortly.

In the "Business" section of the 10-K, we learn more relevant information about Costco's business and strategy. This information is not critical, but it does give us a better understanding of how the company operates. In the next section titled, "Properties," we see a listing of Costco's properties worldwide. The information here should provoke two immediate questions for the reader to ask.

First, since Costco operates 327 warehouse clubs in the United States, can Costco continue to expand the business? Can the U.S. population support more than 327 Costco warehouses? An item of information that we should consider is the company's statement on the previous page, that there are currently over 1,100 warehouse clubs in the United States and Canada operated by Costco, Wal-Mart, and others. A reasonable answer to this question would be that with over 300 million people in the U.S. and Canada, a population of this size should be able to support more than 1,100 warehouse-style stores (nearly 300,000 people per store).

A second question that should come to mind is, "What are investors paying per Costco store?" This can be a slightly involved calculation, but for our purposes I will keep it very basic. We simply divide the market capitalization ("market cap") of Costco (*The market capitalization is the total value of the company which is calculated by multiplying the number of shares outstanding by the price per share*) by the number of Costco warehouse stores (417 worldwide). Costco has approximately 460 million shares of stock outstanding (*this number is found in the income statement, located further on in the 10-K*) and the current share price is approximately $45. Multiplying these two figures produces a market capitalization of about $21 billion. Dividing this amount by the number of stores operated by the company—417—shows that each store is being valued at about $50 million by the stock market. This may seem to the "naked eye" a bit high, but certainly not outrageous (these are not your corner convenience stores, after all). As we shall see later on, there are more useful items to look at when looking at the valuation of Costco. But for right now, we have a rough ballpark figure—we are considering investing in a company where each store is selling for approximately $50 million. Maybe a good price, but maybe too high. Our job is to do more investigating to reach a conclusion.

The next section, Item 3, discusses current legal proceedings against the company. Although it is very difficult for the average investor to draw conclusions from this section of the 10-K, it is worthwhile to at least read it and see if there any obvious material legal proceedings that may threaten the company, such as asbestos or major environmental, price-fixing, or criminal proceedings. Looking at Costco's discussion, it would appear that while Costco is named as a defendant in several lawsuits, they appear to be fairly typical for a company with expansive operations and more than 100,000 employees and millions of customers.

The next item of importance to investors in Costco's 10-K is Item 7— Management's Discussion and Analysis of Financial Condition and Results of Operations. As the portfolio manager of decent-sized mutual fund, I often get to meet with the management of companies in which we invest. Most individual investors, however, do not have this opportunity. Management's discussion in the 10-K, although not completely objective and certainly not a true, live questioning of the individuals running the company, often provides the individual investor with useful information and insight. Rather than discuss each item in the Management Discussion section, it is easier to highlight important items that an investor should focus on.

Costco—Sales And Income

Any heading titled, "Key Items for Fiscal Year 2004," is probably worth a look. What we see here is just that—key operating metrics for a retailer such as Costco. The increase in sales is important and positive, but the more critical number for a retailer is the statistic known as comparable same store sales or "comps." You can see that comps for fiscal 2004 were up 10%, a very impressive figure!

Comp increases are more meaningful than total sales increases for several reasons. A retailer can increase sales simply by opening more stores. However, to increase sales by opening more stores involves constructing or leasing more buildings and hiring more employees, etc. Those additional sales may not be profitable given the huge additional costs that are undertaken to achieve them. An increase in comps, however, entails very little in additional costs other than the cost of the merchandise itself. These additional sales (the increase from year 1 to year 2) are likely to be very profitable. In addition, **when a company is able to increase comps year after year, it is proof that the retailing concept continues to be relevant and appealing to consumers.** Very often, a company can hide weak performance by rapidly opening new stores and showing large sales increases. Investors need to focus on the comp numbers to see if individual stores are actually showing sales increases from one year to the next.

Several lines below the reference to sales, the company states that **Gross Margin** *improved three basis points* (three basis points are .03 of 1 pct or .03%). While three basis points is a very small number, it is an improvement and any improvement in margins is a good thing. *Gross margin* is the amount left over after the cost of goods sold (what Costco itself paid for merchandise) is subtracted from sales (what Costco's customers paid for that same merchandise). Many other expense items such as wages, rent, insurance, etc. are deducted from the gross margin before arriving at the net margin and net income.

It is important to remember that the gross margin can change from one year to the next for reasons beyond management's control. For example, Costco sells various types of merchandise from food to jewelry. Generally, merchandise such as food has a very low markup; jewelry has a very high markup. If Costco were to sell far more food in 2004 versus 2003 and less jewelry, sales might increase, but gross margin and ultimately profitability would probably be lower in 2004 versus 2003. So, while the increase in gross margin of 3 basis points is positive, it is helpful to know if this was achieved through a different mix of merchandise sold, or through other means, such as buying products from suppliers at lower costs or charging customers higher prices, or a combination of the two.

It is important to note that, generally, we do not want to see companies increasing profits by charging customers more. While it is good for a business to have pricing power, more often than not, raising prices is something that can only be done once or just a few times before consumers start to look elsewhere. In the 1980's, cereal companies such as Kellogg's and General Mills showed rapidly rising earnings as they increased prices for their cereals by double-digit amounts year after year. Eventually, consumers got sticker shock when faced with four dollar boxes of cereal and began buying generic brand cereals or simply stopped having cereal for breakfast. Eventually, General Mills and Kelloggs had to lower prices to regain customers and profits dropped dramatically, as did the stock prices.

Toward the bottom of the page, we see that net income increased over 22 percent from the prior year to $1.85 per share. The 22 percent increase in net income from the previous year is impressive, but we must do further investigative work to determine if this increase reflects a fair comparison with the previous year. For example, certain one-time items may have hurt the prior year or artificially boosted the current year, making comparisons unfair and not very meaningful. Such one-time items might include a change in the tax rate from one year to the next. If 2003's tax rate on income was 40 percent and in 2004 it dropped to 30 percent, then that is something we would like to know when determining Costco's true rate of earnings growth.

> For example, if Mr. Smith earned $100 in 2003 and it was taxed at 40% by the government, his net income was $60. In 2004, if Mr. Smith's salary is unchanged at $100, but new tax laws require him to pay only 30% of his income in taxes, his net income in 2004 will be $70. Although his net income increased over 15% from 2003 to 2004, has his income or earnings power really grown? Of course not. The same holds true for corporations. As investors, we want to see real growth; growth in sales, profits, **and** net income.

These are items that we will look for as we continue to go through the 10-K. As far as the earnings of $1.85, we divide the share price of $45 by this amount to calculate the company's **price to earnings**, or **P/E ratio**. In this case, that ratio is just over 24. This seems a bit high (please see later discussion of valuation and P/E), but there are other metrics by which we will attempt to value Costco and we will see if this P/E of 24 is justified.

The final item, referring to the dividend, indicates that the Board of Directors (the individuals elected by the shareholders to "watch over" management and the company) declared a ten cent dividend to be paid each quarter; in other words, 40 cents per share per year. Given that the share price of Costco is approximately $45 per share, this 40 cent dividend represents a yield of just under 1 percent, slightly lower than the average stock in the S&P 500, which yields about 2.1 percent. A low dividend is not necessarily a bad thing if the company is growing and instead of using its cash to pay a dividend, uses it instead to invest in and expand the business.

As we look further down Item 7, we see that some of the data presented, such as income and sales, we have seen earlier. One new bit of useful information that we see under the *"Net Sales"* heading is that while sales were up 13.1% in 2004, 78% of this increase is the result of the increase in same store sales (comps) while the other 22% was the result of new stores. This is significant and positive data. This bit of information is telling us that Costco is growing primarily because its existing stores are attracting more customers and selling more products.

As discussed earlier, the comp sales are more profitable to Costco than the increased sales that come from opening new stores. More importantly, these increased same store sales are a good indication that Costco's warehouse stores are a successful concept—customers are returning in increasing numbers—and likely has staying power. It is good to know that these comps are the primary driver of sales and earnings growth and that the company is not overly dependent on opening new stores (an activity that takes lots of money and management time and will quickly lead to an over-saturation of stores, the condition where there are more Costco stores than the population can support).

The next item that is of interest to us, as investors, is the discussion of selling, general and administrative expenses—S,G &A. While expenses in 2004 were higher than the previous year (which you would expect in a growing business), it is important to note that SG&A expenses, as a percent of sales, are slightly lower than the prior year. What makes this important is that it shows that the business is scalable. What we mean by scalable is that as the business grows, it operates more efficiently and a greater percentage of sales revenue drops to the bottom line as profits. As investors, what we want are increasing profits. The concept of scalability and increased efficiency relates to the theory that eventually the **law of large numbers** catches up with most companies. What I mean by the law of large numbers is that it is common for a company with $10 million in sales to increase sales by 20% for several consecutive years, first to $12 million, then to $14.4 million, and then $17.3 million the year after. Eventually, however, when the company hits, say $1 billion in sales, it will be incredibly difficult to add the same 20 percent in sales increases in subsequent years. While it was not too hard to add $2 million to a $10 million base, it is far harder to add $200 million to a $1 billion base.

One common mistake of investors when analyzing at a company, is that they assume that current growth rates will continue forever and often pay too much for a company's stock. While a fast growing technology company or a hot retailer may be doubling sales and profits from one year to the next, that phenomenon is unlikely to continue for extended periods of time. Given the law of large numbers, it is important to see that a company is becoming more efficient so that while sales growth may drop from 20 to perhaps 18 percent, the company can still continue to increase profits by 20 percent or more. So.… Going back to SG&A, and the importance of it decreasing as a percentage of sales and the reason it is critical to see this decrease, is that it shows that company and its employees are becoming more efficient and can increase profits at a rate higher than the increase in sales. Because the law of large numbers dictates that large sales increases cannot continue indefinitely, we want to see increased operating efficiency, which will allow for continuing high rates of profit growth even as sales growth begins to slow.

The next several paragraphs that refer to Pre-Opening Expenses and Impaired Assets and Closing Costs are not terribly important to our analysis. The paragraphs that follow these items, however, are very significant despite the limited space that is devoted to their presentation.

The first, and more important item, is the discussion of Interest Expense and Interest Income. What is particularly noteworthy about the discussion of interest, is that interest income exceeds interest expense by a substantial amount, approximately $15 million. To earn $15 million of interest income in 2004's very low interest rate environment, must mean that Costco had a lot more cash than debt. We will investigate this shortly. It is also important to note is that interest income jumped from $38.525 million in 2003 to $51.627 million in 2004. This tells us that the company's cash balance grew significantly in the past twelve months to be able to generate this much increased interest income. This tells us that Costco's business is generating large amounts of excess cash—a very good thing. We will investigate this and its ramifications in further detail when we examine the company's Statement of Cash Flows that appears later in the 10-K.

Lastly, what we see just below the discussion of interest expense, is the statement that, "income taxes were 37.0% in 2004 versus 37.5% in 2003"—the tax rate was essentially flat from year to year. It is important to note this. Often a company's earnings will appear to increase substantially from one year to the next, and it is only upon further investigation that we see that it was all due to a lower tax rate. A change in the tax rate is generally considered a one-time event that will likely not occur again. We want to compare earnings from one year to the next on an "apples to apples" basis. Often this is done by comparing pre-tax income from one year to the next. As we discussed earlier, a decrease in the tax rate does not produce a real increase in net income. Tax rates should not be ignored by investors, but we are much more interested in pre-tax earnings power (for example, our salary). Tax rates are somewhat arbitrary and can change from one year to the next.

Cash Flows

As we continue to follow Management's Discussion and Analysis, we will read it in conjunction with the financial statements that are shown in Section IV of the 10-K. When we read the sections addressing Liquidity and Capital Resources and Cash Flows, we need to also look at the Statement of Cash Flows in Section IV.

First, let's start off by defining cash flows. We hear the term quite a bit, "we are having a cash flow problem", "the business is experiencing good cash flow...." What does that mean? Is money flowing? I remember once seeing a nice yacht with the name, "Negative Cash Flow" painted across the transom. An appropriate name, since the cost of buying the boat and keeping it running certainly would be a huge drain on cash. Simply stated, cash flows are the movement of money in and out of the business' bank account. Money flows in from sales and flows out for any expense that the business may incur—to purchase inventory, pay salaries, construct new facilities, etc.

The flow of cash into and out of a business is critical. Often, a company may be earning profits but losing cash (and a business can lose cash for only so long before it forced to close its doors). Enron had profits for several consecutive years immediately before it collapsed. However, an examination of its Statement of Cash Flows would have shown that the company was losing cash year after year despite the reported accounting profits. How can this be? Aren't profits cash? No. Profits are the reported numbers that are calculated using various accounting methods. Generally, companies with annual profits are financially healthy and earning cash, but not always. Our job, as analysts, is to avoid being fooled into investing in a company that appears profitable but is in fact in bad shape because it is bleeding cash.

How can a profitable company lose cash? Here is an example—I open a restaurant. It shows some early promise and I decide that the way to really make a lot of money is to open up a small chain of similar restaurants. To do so, I borrow $5 million dollars from the bank to open ten more restaurants. The $5 million I borrowed is spent signing new leases, purchasing equipment, tables, chairs, silverware and food. Now I have eleven restaurants and after a year, my accountant tells me that they earned a combined profit of $500,000 (total sales were $2 million and expenses were $1.5 million).

But, when computing profits, only certain items are deducted as expenses, mostly items that are considered "consumables"—food, salaries, rent, etc. The money that I spent on the restaurant equipment is not considered an expense for accounting purposes. If it is a long lasting asset, it is considered a *capital expenditure* and only a small portion of that amount can be deducted each year as *depreciation* of that equipment. In year two of operating my restaurants, I hear complaints that customers have to wait a long time for their meals to arrive. It turns out that I do not have large enough stoves and ovens in the restaurants. I need to spend an additional $1 million to expand the cooking facilities. So I use my profits from last year of $500,000 and return to the bank and borrow another $500,000 to come up with the million dollars. At the end of year two, my accountant tells me that the restaurants earned profits of $600,000. (Sales of $2.2 million less expenses of $1.6 million.) But notice what happened in year two—profits were $600,000 but my cash balance is now less than it was at the end of year one, plus I now owe the bank $5.5 million up $500,000 from year one. So what is going on??? My accountant is telling me that the restaurants are earning profits but my cash flow is negative. This can only continue for a few years before I am forced to go out of business (likely to occur when the $5.5 million loan from the bank comes due).

Certainly, new, rapidly growing business are often cash flow negative, but after several years of operating, we would like to see the business generating cash—that is, more cash is ending up in the bank than is leaving to fund expansion. When more cash is leaving than is coming in, the shortfall is often made up by borrowing, which can put the business in a very risky position should growth ever slow or should the bank ever decide to stop lending money or call in the debt.

Ideally, what we want to see are accounting profits *and* cash flow coming in which increases the amount of cash that we have at the bank. If our business is building its cash balance at the bank, as owners we can eventually take some of that cash for ourselves and buy the home we always wanted, pay for our children's college or maybe take a nice vacation.

As investors in shares of company stock, we are owners of a small portion of that business. If a company has 100 million shares outstanding and we purchase 100 shares as an investment, we own one/one-millionth of that company. If cash is going to be returned to the owners of the company (the shareholders), we are going to get our one/one-millionth of that cash. A one-one millionth ownership interest may sound ridiculously small, but if the company is paying $500 million to shareholders in a given year through a dividend payout, that is $500 for us. Not bad for owning 100 shares.

So…. a bit of a long winded-discussion of cash flow versus straight accounting earnings, but I hope you understand the importance of positive cash flow to us as investors in (owners of) the business. Let us look at Costco's cash flows and see what they tell us about Costco's attractiveness as a possible investment. In other words—do we want to be owners of Costco, entitled to a fractional share of these cash flows?

The Statement of Cash Flows shows the movement of cash in and out of the company's bank account. The first section shows the inflows (hopefully they are inflows) of cash from operating activities—in Costco's case, from operating its warehouse stores. The cash flows from operating activities start with "net income" and then adds or subtracts other items that affected cash in the bank. For example, the depreciation expense is added back to net income. Although depreciation is an expense by accounting standards, it does not affect cash. For example, even though the car we own is depreciating in value with every passing year, no cash leaves our wallet as a result. However, at the end of ten years, we need a new car and we buy one—that is when the cash leaves our bank account. That outflow appears in the next section—cash flows (usually outflows) from investing activities.

Investing activities are generally expenditures for expanding the business such as building or purchasing new buildings, equipment, or the acquisition of another business. For a company to have excess or "free cash flow" inflows from operating activities must exceed outflows from investing activities. In my previous restaurant example, the problem with my restaurant business was that investing outflows each year far exceeded the inflows from operating activities. That cannot continue for too long before the business collapses.

The third item on the cash flow statement is, "Cash Flows from Financing Activities". Items that fall under this heading are such things as the borrowing or repayment of bank debt, the sale or repurchase of shares of stock and the payment of dividends to shareholders.

If we were to look at our household finances and construct a statement of cash flows for it, our cash flows from operating activities would include our wages from our job less items for such things as food, rent gifts, entertainment, etc. Hopefully, the sum of these items would be a positive number and that would be the total for cash flows from operations. Cash Flows from investing activities would include such items as the purchase of a house or car. And lastly, cash flows from financing activities would include such items as mortgage payments or auto payments.

We all have a pretty good grasp of our own personal or household financial condition. If you think of a company in the same dimension as your personal financial situation, it will be easier to logically see which companies are on solid financial grounds and which may be houses of cards destined to implode.

Corporate Statement of Cash Flows		Household Statement of Cash Flows	
Operating Cash Flow		**Operating Cash Flow**	
Net Income	$250,000	Salary	$100,000
Add:Depreciation	$40,000	Rent	-$20,000
Change in accounts receivable	-$6,000	Food	-$8,000
Change in accounts payable	$4,000	Fuel/Travel/Leisure	-$10,000
Total Operating Cash Flow	$288,000	Total Operating Cash Flow	$62,000
Cash Flows from Investing		**Cash Flows From Investing**	
Purchase of Heavy Equip.	-$30,000	Purchase of new car	-$24,000
(capital expenditures)			
Purchase of Building	-$80,000		
Purchase of XYZ Co.	-$150,000		
Cash Flows from Financing		**Cash Flows from Financing**	
Sale of bonds, proceeds used	$80,000	Repayment of credit card debt	-$10,000
Dividends paid to shareholders	-$80,000		
Free Cash Flow	$28,000	Free Cash Flow	$28,000

Note that free cash flow for a household is the amount of money that can be put into the bank in a given year. For the corporation, free cash flow is also the excess cash generated each year that can be used to pay out a dividend, repurchase shares of stock, or simply put in the bank.

Armed with this understanding of cash flow, let's look at Costco's Statement of Cash Flows. We see that Costco's total net cash inflows from operating activities for the year ended 8/29/2004 (*the fiscal year*[1]) was $2.098 billion. Costco used just over $1 billion for investing activities. Most of this money was used to purchase new buildings and equipment. Costco also took in some cash from its financing activities but this item is not essential to our analysis and I will not devote much time to examining it.

It is important for investors to look at the Finance section in the Statement of Cash Flows to see if the company has taken on substantial amounts of new debt (generally not a good thing) or sold more shares or repaid large amounts of debt (a good thing) or repurchased large amounts of stock, (generally a good thing since the company is using its own cash to purchase its own shares. Basically, management is saying that it believes the company's share price is undervalued and purchasing its own shares with its extra cash implies that management believes that the company's stock is a good investment.) In Costco's case, there were no significant purchases or sales of debt or stock, so we will focus solely on the Cash Flows from Operating and Investing Activities.

Free Cash Flow

The important information to take away from Costco's Statement of Cash Flows is that in 2004 Costco took in $2,098,783,000 from operating activities and spent $705,620,000 on capital expenditures to expand and maintain the retail business. What is left over is the Amount of **Free Cash Flow** for the company.

Free cash flow is what is left over after the company meets all its operating expenses (wages, insurance, supplies, etc) and capital expenditures ("capex"— new buildings, upgrades, machinery, etc). It is what we, in our household, have left over after we take in our salary and pay all of our expenses and capex (new car, shed, lawn tractor, etc). As we know from personal experience, it is good to have excess cash left over at the end of the year. The same thing applies for a company. *Free cash flow is a good thing!*

---

[1] *Fiscal year—not all companies follow the standard January-December calendar. A company can use any day of the year to begin its "fiscal" year. In Costco's case, its year for record—keeping purposes, begins on August 30, and ends on August 29th of the following year. It is not important to devote too much time to why companies elect to use dates that differ from the standard calendar. Investors only need to be aware that such situations are fairly common.*

Our job is to measure the amount of free cash flow and determine what is a significant or meaningful amount of free cash flow. The amount in dollars is important, but we want to see how much free cash there is relative to the company's size. In Costco's case, free cash flow looks to be about $1.4 billion ($2,098,783,000 minus $705,620,000 = $1,393,163,000). This may seem like a huge amount of free cash flow. While it is an impressive sum, it is important to remember that Costco is a $21 billion company.[2] (*A company's size is the same as its market capitalization, which for Costco = $45 dollar share price x approx. 480 million shares outstanding = approx. $21 billion.*)

How should we look at the free cash flow relative to the size of Costco? I like to look at what is known as the **Free Cash Flow Yield**—the free cash flow yield is the free cash flow, in dollars, divided by the market cap of the company. In this case *the free cash flow yield is 1,393 divided by 21,000 = .066 or 6.6%.* In other words, Costco's free cash flow equals a yield of 6.6% of the total market value (market cap.) of the company. This is a difficult but an important concept to understand. Here's why—we are not just focusing on what stocks to buy with our investment money. We are considering what stocks to buy versus other types of investment opportunities—bonds, real estate or an alpaca farm.

Let us look at the concept of free cash flow yield as it applies to real estate. After all, the value of any asset or investment is the value of the cash that it earns for the owner/investor. Assume an apartment building cost $1 million (that is the market cap or the market value of the apartment building—same as the market cap of a company like Costco—basically what it would cost to acquire an entire property or company). Assume that we buy the building with 100% cash—the same way we buy stocks. The annual rent from the apartments in 2004 was $120,000. The expenses associated with the building in 2004 (repairs, heat, property taxes, etc) were $80,000. The remaining $40,000 is the free cash flow for the year. $40,000 divided by the purchase price, or market cap. of $1,000,000, = a free cash flow yield of 4%.

Now look at the free cash flow yield of a U.S. Government Treasury Bond. If we buy $100,000 of U.S. Treasury bonds that pay interest of 3.5% per year, our cash flow (yes, operating cash flow) is $3,500 per year. Our expenses are zero, so the free cash flow from this bond investment is also $3,500 and the free cash

---

2   *A company's "size" is the same as its market capitalization (market cap). The market cap is simply the number of shares outstanding multiplied by the price per share. The size and market cap are theoretically the amount of money it would take to purchase every share of stock that a corporation has outstanding, and in effect, own 100% of that company.*

flow yield is the same as the yield on the bonds—3.5%. Every investment—stocks, real estate, bonds, can be seen as having a free cash flow yield.

How does this help us evaluate Costco's 6.6% free cash flow yield? It would be helpful to determine if free cash flow is increasing from year to year, decreasing, or relatively flat. Looking at 2003 on the Statement of Cash Flows, we see that Cash Flows from Operations was approx. $1.507 billion while capital expenditures (additions to property and equipment) were approx. $810 million resulting in free cash flow of roughly $700 million. In 2002, free cash flow was actually slightly negative (CFO of $1.018 billion less capex of $1.028 billion). So, free cash flow would appear to be increasing substantially from year to year. It is important to remember that three years is a relatively small sample, but nonetheless, there does appear to be a trend. As the company opens new warehouse clubs and existing warehouse clubs increase sales from one year to the next (remember those same store comps!), cash flow from operations increases from one year to the next. As Costco matures, the need to open more and more stores subsides and the company spends less each year in capex to open new stores. This combination leads to increasing free cash flow from year to year. Successful mature businesses are often referred to as free cash flow cows—the businesses may not be growing at a rapid pace but they generate large amounts of free cash flow for investors/owners.

To get back to our original question, "Is Costco's 6.6% free cash flow yield a good yield?" Given the information we have, the answer appears to be YES. A yield of 6.6% sounds pretty respectable on its own, especially since the yield on other investments such as bonds, bank CDs, or real estate, is currently a lot less than 6.6%. Based on the trends we see in the 10-K, it is reasonable to believe that free cash flow in 2005 will be even higher than 2004. Perhaps the yield may reach 7.5 or 8% next year.

This increasing yield points out an important difference between stocks and bonds. When an investor purchases bonds that yield 5%, that 5% income yield does not change from year to year. Each year the investor gets his or her 5% interest payment—no more, no less. (They are called *fixed*-income investments for a reason!) Upon maturity, the principal is returned to the investor. With a stock, however, there is the possibility that the yield or income from the stock will continually increase from one year to the next. In addition, there is also the possibility that the stock will increase in price over time. The tradeoff, however, is that while the bondholder knows with some degree of certainty that he will get his investment principal returned to him when the bonds mature, the shareholder must rely on the company continuing to do well to keep the stock price at or above what the investor paid for the stock when he purchased it.

Dividends

What you are probably asking yourself is, "OK, so Costco has a free cash flow yield of 6.6%, but how do I as a shareholder get paid any of this cash??" Generally, a corporation has no legal obligation to return excess cash to shareholders. However, management's goal in running the corporation is to maximize the value of the business. That maximization is accomplished by increasing the share price of the company's stock.

A company will often use its cash in the bank to get its share price higher. How does this occur? The most common method is through a dividend. Many companies pay dividends to shareholders, usually quarterly. Shareholders value these payments since they are a form of income (a return of cash) to the shareholder. The ability of a company to pay a dividend depends of how much excess or free cash it has to return to shareholders. A company with significant free cash can pay a fairly high dividend to shareholders.

Companies that are in slow growth businesses such as utilities or food companies generally pay high dividends to shareholders since it has little need to use the excess cash to try to grow the business. For example, no matter how much Con Edison or Pacific Gas & Electric spends or invests, it is unlikely to get its customers to use more of its products—gas and electricity—they are stuck in a slow-growing industry. It is a better use of excess cash to pay shareholders. Shareholders who receive dividend payments of 3% (dividend payment divided by share price), 4% or more, will find buying and/or holding the shares a more attractive investment than bonds or bank CDs, which also make regular payments to holders in the form of interest. A dividend will also help hold up the price of the stock. For example if a stock that is trading for $30 per share pays a dividend of $1 per year (25 cents each quarter) its yield would be 3.33% ($30 dividend by $1). The share price is unlikely to drop too severely because if the price were to drop to $20, the yield would now be 5% ($20 divided by the same $1). Investors would find this yield very attractive when compared to bonds, CDs and other dividend paying stocks. If the stock price were ever to approach $20, it is likely that investors would rush in to buy the stock, sending the share price back up. It should be noted, though, that if the company's business has suffered, and cash flow is expected to be lower in the years ahead, investors may worry that the current dividend of $1 may be reduced or eliminated entirely if the company's cash flow cannot support the annual dividend payment.

One example of such a situation involves Philip Morris (now known as Altria Corp.) Philip Morris' main businesses, cigarettes (Marlboro), food (Entenmann's, Birds Eye, etc) and Miller Beer are mature, slow-growing businesses but they generate tremendous amounts of free cash flow. In the 1990's investors began to be concerned that the company might be forced to pay huge amounts of monetary damages to smokers who could show that they were made ill by Philip Morris' cigarettes. The share price dropped sharply. Philip Morris management tried to get the share price higher by raising the dividend. At times, the dividend yield of Philip Morris stock was higher than 7%. Investors were not biting at the big dividend, though, since they worried that eventually the company would be forced to pay huge damages resulting from lawsuits and the large dividend might soon disappear.

At present we see a similar situation with shares of General Motors, whose shares have a dividend yield of more than 8%. This yield has not been able to support the share price as investors worry that the company will be forced to cut the dividend as it continues to lose money in its auto manufacturing operations. However, if a business and its prospects are healthy, a dividend will help to hold up the price of the company's stock.

Apart from special situations such as Philip Morris and General Motors, a rise in a company's dividend usually brings about a rise in the company's stock price. Recent tax law changes lowered the tax rate for income received in the form of dividends. Income earned from dividends is now taxed at a lower rate than most income received from salary and wages. The important point to remember is that a company with free cash flow can afford to pay a dividend. A company with increasing free cash flow can afford to continually increase the dividend that it pays, which will go a long way to keeping the share price rising in the future. Increasing free cash flow from one year to the next often leads to an increasing dividend over time, which often causes a company's stock price to rise, making it a good investment. Lastly, and perhaps most importantly, the dividend is the primary mechanism by which investors can receive much of the free cash flow that their corporation is earning.

Share Repurchases

Another way that a company can use its free cash flow to support its stock price is by using excess cash to repurchase some of its outstanding shares. This is a slightly less obvious concept than the dividend issue but nearly as important. The best way to explain it is through an example.

A company can use its cash to expand its business or to purchase a competing business or also to purchase its own stock. Why would a company want to purchase shares of itself? Hopefully this example will explain. Assume that company XYZ has 1,000 shares of stock outstanding and each share is currently trading for $50 per share. Last year the company earned $5,000, or $5 per share ($5,000 divided by 1,000 shares = $5 per share). The company's business is strong but investors, for some reason, are not rushing out to buy the shares and the stock has been stuck around $50 for quite some time. The business is going well but investors are only valuing the company at a price to earnings ratio of ten. (The *price to earnings ratio is the stock price divided by earnings per share—in this case it is $50 divided by $5 = 10*). Since the business is solid, the company has been generating free cash flow for the past several years. The money has just been sitting in the bank and has not helped increase the share price. The cash balance in the bank now stands at $5,000.

Management decides to use this money to buy back shares of the company to get the share price higher. How will this help the share price? Let's see— Currently there are 1,000 shares outstanding, selling at $50 per share and the company is earning $5,000 per year, or $5 per share, for price earnings ratio of 10. Management takes the $5,000 sitting in the bank and purchases 100 shares and retires them. Now there are only 900 shares outstanding instead of 1,000. The year's total earnings of $5,000 are now spread out over only 900 shares. Earnings per share are now $5.56 per share ($5,000 divided by 900 shares). If investors still value this company at ten times earnings, the shares should now sell for $55.60. If the stock continues to trade at $50, management will use next years free cash flow to buy in and retire more shares until year after year there will fewer and fewer shares outstanding.

Splitting the earnings of the company among fewer and fewer shares means much higher earnings for each share. It is like a pizza pie—fewer and fewer slices of the pie mean bigger individual pieces. Eventually, after many years, if there are only ten shares outstanding and earnings are still $5,000 (more likely, after many years, total earnings will be more than $5,000 if the company is growing at all), those ten shares would have earnings per share of $500 each. If the price to earnings ratio remained around ten, the shares would trade for thousands of dollars each.

Think of fewer shares outstanding as each share being worth more. Again, back to our real estate analogy. A $1/10^{th}$ interest in a house is far more valuable than a $1/1,000^{th}$ interest. That is why a company buying back shares and retiring them, increases the value of the shares that remain outstanding. Once again, free cash flow is a good thing. It can be used in more than one way to increase the share price and turn a middling investment into a profitable venture.

Applying this lesson to our analysis of Costco, what do we see? Costco generated approximately $1.4 billion of free cash flow in 2004 after generating nearly $700 million of free cash flow in 2003. So where is that money? Turn back a few pages in the 10-K and find Costco's consolidated balance sheet. The balance sheet shows all the assets (cash, inventory, buildings, etc) and liabilities (usually debt) of the company. Look at Costco's cash balance—it is over $2.8 billion dollars. Wow! That is a lot of cash. All that cash must be good for share-holders, right? Let's reflect on the two examples from above—it looks likes Costco could pay us a pretty decent dividend if they wanted to—based on last year's free cash flow alone of $1.4 billion, it looks like Costco could pay each share (remember there are 480 million shares outstanding) a dividend of nearly $3 (1.4 billion divided by 480 million = 2.92). Based on the current share price of $45 that is nearly a 7% yield. Wow, that is lot more than my bank is paying me to hold my money.[3]

What else can Costco do? They could buy back a lot of shares and increase the value of the remaining shares outstanding. Let's see how this would work—Costco could take $2 billion of its $2.8 billion of cash in the bank and buy back over 44 million shares of stock ($2 billion divided by $45 (the price per share) = 44.444 million). The number of shares outstanding would drop from 480 million to 436 million shares. Last year's earnings of $882.393 million would now be split among 436 million shares instead of 480. Earnings per share would now be $2.02 ($882 million divided by 436 million), instead of the $1.85 that was reported. If the stock is to continue selling at a price earnings ratio of 24 (45 divided by 1.85), the share price should increase to $48.48 (24 times $2.02). Remember, the pie is being cut into fewer pieces. The size of the pie remains the same, so each slice (share price) should be bigger.

The Balance Sheet

Having focused on Costco's cash flow and its importance, we now turn our attention to the company's balance sheet and it's implication for our invest-ment decision—whether or not to buy Costco stock. **A balance sheet lists the assets and liabilities of a company.** On one side of the balance sheet are assets—items that the company owns or is owed, such as cash, buildings, accounts receivable etc. On the other side of the balance sheets are liabilities and the shareholder's equity in the business. Liabilities include items such as debt and accounts payable.

---

[3]   *Readers should note that on page 9 of the 10-K, under Dividend Policy, the company states that under the terms of its credit agreements, Costco is restricted from paying more than 50% of its net income—$1.85 per share in 2004—in dividends. However, the borrowings under these credit agreements are relatively small and it would be fairly simple for Costco to use some of its cash to close out the credit agreements and free itself of the dividend restrictions.*

The assets and liabilities plus shareholder's equity will always equal each other. In other words they will *balance*, hence the name, balance sheet. It may seem strange to include assets on one side and liabilities *plus* owner's equity on the other. After all, isn't owner's equity an asset? Yes, but not exactly. Let look at our household finances as a balance sheet. If we had to list our household net worth as a balance sheet, it might appear as follows:

Assets		Liabilities + Owner's Equity	
Cash in bank	$5,000	Mortgage Debt on house	$70,000
House	$100,000	Loan for Auto	$10,000
Auto	$15,000	Credit Card Debt	$5,000
Stamp collection	$3,000	Total Liabilities	$85,000
Furniture	$10,000	Owner's Equity	$58,000
Clothing, jewelry, etc	$10,000		
Total Assets	$143,000	Total Liabilities and Owner's Equity	$143,000

Notice that *Owner's Equity* is the difference between the value of the assets that you have and the amount of debt outstanding that was used to buy them. Makes sense—if you own a home that is worth two million dollars but you took out a $1.5 million dollar mortgage loan to buy it, you are not really a millionaire. You are worth the value of the asset, $2 million, minus the amount of debt owed, $1.5 million. Your net worth, or owner's equity, is $500,000. Now that we have a general idea of what a balance sheet shows, let's take a look at Costco's.

The balance sheet presents Costco's assets and liabilities at the close of the company's fiscal year, August 29, 2004. It also compares the current year's figures with last year's. What we want to determine from the balance sheet is:

> "How stable is this company?"
> "Is debt increasing from year to year and will the company be
> able to pay the debt when it comes due?"
> "Does the company have a lot of cash in the bank that can be
> used to benefit shareholders?"

Let's see what we can learn from Costco's balance sheet.

The first line under Assets—Current Assets, is "cash and cash equivalents." Note that *Costco has over $2.8 billion of cash in the bank* or in cash equivalents such as short-term U.S. government bonds. More importantly, note that this $2.8 billion balance is nearly $1.3 billion higher than one year ago. How did cash increase so much from a year from a year ago. Remember our earlier discussion of Costco's free cash flow? We showed from the Statement of Cash Flows that Costco had nearly $1.4 billion of free cash flow in 2004. Here is where that money ended up. It is sitting in the bank or invested in short-term bonds, waiting to be put to good use (we hope—and that is why a good management team is so important).

When we look at how much cash a company has, we immediately want to see how that amount of cash compares with the amount of debt the company has borrowed. Looking down the balance sheet, we see that Costco has a minimal amount of short-term borrowings ($21.5 million) and nearly *$994 million of long-term debt.* Is this a lot of debt for a company of Costco's size? Simply put, no. This a miniscule amount of debt for a company with an equity (stock) market capitalization of over $20 billion. More importantly, though, remember that Costco has over $2.8 billion of cash in the bank. The company could pay off all its outstanding debt simply by writing a check. In addition, Costco had $1.4 billion of free cash flow in 2004 and since the trend indicates that free cash flow is increasing, it seems likely that Costco will have at least $1.4 billion of free cash flow in 2005. Even if the company did not want to disturb the cash that it has sitting in the bank, Costco could simply repay all of its debt from cash that should come in during 2005. Simply put, Costco has very little debt relative to its size, free cash flow, and amount of cash in the bank. *Costco would appear to be on very secure financial ground.*

Using Assets On The Balance Sheet To Increase The Stock Price

What else can we learn from Costco's balance sheet? Remember earlier that I mentioned steps a company can take to use its cash flow to increase share price. In this instance, Costco can utilize its large cash horde to increase its share price. With over $2.8 billion in cash and 480 million shares outstanding, *Costco has over $5.80 in cash for each share outstanding.* Costco currently pays a dividend of 46 cents per share each year (11.5 cents each quarter), for a yield of just over 1 %. *Costco could probably increase that dividend by over $1 per year and perhaps pay a dividend of $1.50 per share per year.* With a $1.50 dividend, the yield on Costco stock would jump to over 3.3% and would probably cause investors to bid the share price higher. How does a stock get bid higher? Simply, more investors rush out to buy the shares than there are shareholders willing to sell. When there are more buyers than sellers, prices rise. Pretty simple.

What else can Costco do with its cash to increase the share price? As we mentioned earlier, with $2.8 billion of cash and a share price of approximately 45, Costco could repurchase and retire over 60 million shares of stock. After this repurchase there would only be 420 million shares outstanding instead of the current 480 million. Earnings per share would rise as the total earnings are divided among fewer shares (remember our pizza slices analogy). 2004's income of $882 million (the pie) divided by only 420 million shares (fewer slices) would produce earnings per share of $2.10 (bigger slices) instead of the $1.85 per share earned when the income was divided among the 480 million shares outstanding. Assuming that investors are still willing to pay the same 24 times earnings for Costco stock, the share price could rise to $50.40 (24 x $2.10) after a large 60 million share buyback. Looking at these two possible scenarios, a dividend increase or a large share buyback, *the important thing to take away from the cash on Costco's balance sheet is that the $2.8 billion cash there could be used to increase the share price significantly.*

Miscellaneous Balance Sheet Items

Looking at the remaining items on the balance sheet, nothing seems particularly noteworthy, either good or bad. We see that under current liabilities, the company owes $3.6 billion for accounts payable (merchandise bought but not yet paid for) but this is entirely offset by the $3.6 billion of receivables (items sold where payment has not yet been received—most likely these are credit card sales, where the merchandise has been sold to customers but VISA or Amex has not yet paid Costco).

Costco owes employees salaries of approximately $900 million (it is not that Costco is delinquent in paying its employees. Most likely this amount represents wages owed to employees who have worked in the past several days, but have not yet received their paychecks from the company since paychecks are probably handed out weekly or twice a month) and other current liabilities. Costco's ability to make these payments is hardly in doubt since the company has over $3.6 billion of merchandise (current assets) on its balance sheet (and presumably in the stores as well) that are continuously being sold and converted into cash to meet current payment obligations. In summary, the balance sheet appears very healthy and should not be a source of concern.

Management

Now that we have looked at the major financial statements in the 10-K—Management's Discussion of Income and Expenses, the Statement of Cash Flows, and the Balance Sheet, there are several remaining items in the 2004 Costco 10-K that we should look at before beginning our analysis of whether Costco is likely to be a good stock investment.

On page 26 of the 10-K, a section that is worth reading, is a listing of the Directors and Executive Officers of Costco. While a thorough review of the career histories and backgrounds of Costco's top executive officers would take considerable time and effort, there is a good deal of information available to investors in the company's 10-K. In addition, with information so readily available on the Internet, any investor desiring more information on a particular individual can easily access information using an online search engine such as Yahoo! or Google.

Reviewing the brief bios in the 10-K, we see that the President/CEO, James Sinegal and Chairman, Jeffrey Brotman, are the co-founders of the company and have *more than two decades of experience* with the company. The other top officers listed have been with the company for nearly equally long periods. It appears that Costco has a policy of promoting from within and advancing employees in the organization. Notice, Thomas Walker, an executive vice president, started with Costco in 1983 as an assistant warehouse manager and is now in charge of construction, distribution, and traffic.

Given Costco's solid operating history, it is good to see that the company is cohesive and senior officers have long periods of experience with the company. It is often a bad sign when senior officers have a limited history with the company they manage, or sometimes even limited experience within the same type of industry. Remember, just because a person is the CEO, does not necessarily mean that they are talented. It is important to see a management team, such as Costco's, with a long and successful operating history.

The Proxy Statement—Inside Ownership And Management Compensation

When looking at management, one of the things I like to see is substantial inside ownership—ownership of shares of the company that they manage. I like to see that management is in the same boat as the shareholders. If the chef won't eat his own cooking, we should be concerned. This information is not provided in the 10-K. In Item 12 on page 27 of the 10-K, it states that this information along with executive compensation (another item I like to look at) is provided in the company's Proxy Statement. A Proxy Statement contains information sent to shareholders providing them various items of interest about the company. It also asks them to vote for candidates to serve on the Board of Directors of the company.

It is through the election of the Board of Directors that the shareholders ultimately control the company. Each share owned by a stockholder is entitled to one vote. Stockholders who own a large number of shares can often influence the management of the company through their large number of votes for their own nominees for the Board of Directors. The CEO and other executive officers manage the day to day operations of the company, but the Board of Directors, elected by the shareholders, oversees the executive officers and has the power to fire and replace them. Ironically, the chief executive officer of a corporation is also frequently the chairman of the board of directors. As a result, the Board of Directors is not always the best watchdog over management. Sometimes shareholders need to get directly involved and replace the Board in order to bring about changes in top management.

Looking at Costco's Proxy Statement (the 14A filing, which can be found at: http://www.sec.gov/Archives/edgar/data/909832/000119312504216583/ddef14a.htm) we see on page 6, the list of executive officers and directors and their investment stake in Costco. Notice that the two co-founders (Costco's CEO and Chairman of the Board) own well over two million shares each, nearly five million shares combined, and each own another 1.3 million options on shares. The shares alone are worth over $100 million each at current market prices. We also see that Richard DiCerchio, Costco's chief operating officer, owns shares and options that have a substantial value. Also note that several of Costco's past officers, who are also directors, own large amounts of Costco stock. Presumably, as officers and directors, they know the company very well and if they have the confidence to hold onto their Costco shares, perhaps we should infer that the outlook for the company is favorable.

The second item in the Proxy Statement, that every shareholder should read, is the summary of executive compensation. Generally, I do not like to see top management receiving huge base salaries and ridiculously large bonuses, especially when performance has been less than stellar. Excessive executive compensation is a large problem in the area of corporate governance and for American society as whole. But that is a topic for another time and for now I will focus on the summary of executive compensation in Costco's 14A filing. What we see here is a relatively ideal scenario for shareholders. Note that none of the top executive officers received cash salaries or bonuses in excess of one million dollars for the three years shown. Salaries in the $300-450,000 range may seem high, they are very modest for top officers of a successful public company of this size. The bonuses, none of which exceeded $200,000 is also very modest by prevailing standards. It is equally important, however, that a company not underpay top executives, otherwise talented individuals may leave the firm. What we see in Costco's case, is that while executives receive relatively little cash compensation, they are well-rewarded with options on Costco stock. These option awards to top executives are potentially worth several million dollars to each executive, but only if Costco's share price increases over time. If the share price were to stagnate or decline these options will expire worthless. How are these option awards good for shareholders? The options keep management's goals aligned with shareholders. Everyone is in the same boat. Executives want to run the company as well and as profitably as possible to get the share price to rise so that their options will also rise in value. And that is good for us as investors.

This look at the Proxy Statement is a worthwhile exercise, but few small investors bother with this step. Had more Tyco shareholders bothered to look at the company's 14A, they would have seen that the top officers of that company were receiving huge bonuses of cash and stock. Granted, they would not have seen that Tyco CEO Dennis Kozlowski was wasting company money on Park Avenue apartments, million dollar works of art, and fancy birthday parties for his wife, but they would have seen from the executive compensation disclosures that greed had run amok at the company. Clearly, the Board of Directors was not acting in the best interests of shareholders and a look through the Proxy Statement would have revealed that.

Miscellaneous 10-K Items

Turning back to Costco's 10-K, we need to look at a few remaining items that prospective investors should examine, much of which is standard language boilerplate, but it needs to be examined nonetheless.

The first item is the Report of the Independent Accounting Firm, which appears on page 31 of the 10-K. This report is usually standard language, but should still be examined to ensure that the Report is a clean one and that the accounting firm has not found anything during its audit that would concern investors. The important language to look for, appears in paragraph three, where the auditor, KPMG, states that, "the financial statements … present fairly … the consolidated financial position of Costco Wholesale Corp." While the vast majority of reports from the auditors use this exact same language, there are times when an auditing firm will state that the financial statements of the company in question do not accurately represent the company's financial position—a very big red warning flag. An auditor may also sometimes state that the financial statements cast doubt on the company's ability to continue as a going concern. This may occur when the company's operations are deteriorating rapidly and large amounts of debt may be coming due shortly. These opinions are rare, but when they do appear, should serve as a big neon warning sign to investors. Costco's report, however, is a standard, clean report from its auditors. This is not to say that the auditors are recommending Costco as an investment. The accounting firm is simply stating that the financial statements, for better or worse, accurately reflect the financial condition of the company.

Notes To The Financial Statements

Lastly, we need to read through the Notes to the Consolidated Financial Statements. The Notes are too numerous to go through individually in this book, but it is important that investors read through them and see that they appear reasonable and sound.

While few people can expertly dissect every note in a set of financial statements, most investors with a good amount of common sense can read through the Notes and see if there any items that seem odd or troublesome. Reviewing Costco's Notes, there appear to be no items of major concern. Two items that I will focus on are items related to Costco's debt (page 45), leases (page 48), and items related to stock options (page 50).

In reviewing the Notes related to debt, I look to see that there is not a large amount of debt hidden in subsidiaries that does not appear on Costco's consolidated balance sheet. A review of the bank credit facilities, letters of credit, and short-term facilities, confirms that total debt levels are low and should not pose a risk to the company. Related to debt are the company's leases. The leases, detailed on page 48, are similar to debt in that the rent that the company must pay for its stores each year are fixed obligations, much like debt and interest payments. We see on the schedule on page 48 that lease payments for the next several years approximate $100 million per year through 2009 and total approximately $1 billion for the combined years thereafter. Relative to Costco's income, cash flow, and size of operations, these amounts do not appear excessive.

Lastly, it is always worth examining the number of options that the company has issued to employees and executives. From Note 5 we see that the stock option expense to the company was $36.5 million in 2004 and that there are currently 50.534 million options outstanding with an average strike price of $33.45. The option expense for 2004 does not seem terribly high. However, the 50 million options outstanding represent just over ten percent of the number of shares currently outstanding. If and when these options are eventually converted into shares of Costco stock, it will dilute the existing shareholders. Back to our pizza example, the pie will remain the same size, but the number of slices (shares) will be greater, resulting in each slice being smaller. This is not too great a concern with Costco since the company's huge cash balance can be used to purchase and retire enough stock outstanding to more than offset any dilution from option exercise.

It would be unproductive to go into greater detail on this issue, but investors without significant financial experience should be aware of stock options and how they can dilute the ownership stake of existing shareholders. For example, if Costco, with 480 million of shares outstanding, were to reveal in its notes to the financial statements that there are 200 million options outstanding, that should serve as a red warning flag to investors. Again, it is not critical that investors be able to calculate exactly how dilutive these options will be. It is more important that investors who read this, be aware of what stock options are, and realize that too many of them can hurt existing shareholders down the road when they may eventually be converted into stock.

Cutting To The Chase—Is Costco A Good Stock To Buy?

The Bull (Positive) Argument

Now that we have reviewed Costco's 10-K and looked at the Proxy Statement, how do we use all this information to determine if Costco stock is likely to be a good investment? After gathering all of our data, it is helpful to summarize the positives and negatives, quantify the risks, and estimate what Costco stock is worth. In our analysis of Costco's 10-K and Proxy Statement, there were numerous positive attributes related to the company. I would summarize the more significant ones as follows:

1. Total sales, comparable same stores sales, and earnings are increasing at a very healthy rate. Sales were up 13.1 percent in 2004. Most of the sales increase came from the same store sales increase of 10 percent. New store openings were responsible for the remainder of the sales increase. Profit margins increased, which allowed the 13 percent increase in sales to result in a 22 percent increase in net income for 2004.

2. Costco's free cash flow is impressive, with free cash flow representing 6.6% of the company's market capitalization (6.6% free cash flow yield).

3. The tremendous free cash flow has led to a surplus of cash on the balance sheet, with cash exceeding debt by $1.8 billion. With all this excess cash, Costco can significantly increase its dividend or purchase and retire a significant number of outstanding shares.

4. A purchase of its own shares by the company would increase the value of the shares that remain outstanding.

5. Earnings per share for 2004 would have been nearly ten percent higher if the company chose to use its cash to purchase its own shares during the year.

6. The Proxy Statement highlighted that Costco management is experienced, and executives receive most of their compensation in the form of stock and options, ensuring that their interests are aligned with those of investors.

7. Lastly, we saw that top management has a significant ownership of Costco stock, further ensuring that they will be motivated to perform for stockholders.

The Bear (Negative) Argument

Costco is not without a few weak spots and general risks.

1. Costco operates in a very competitive segment of the retail industry where profit margins are razor thin. In an attempt to constantly deliver the lowest possible prices to its customers, the company is willing to absorb some short-term losses in areas such as the company's gasoline retail operations. This may be a wise decision for the long-term satisfaction of its customers, but in the short-term it can hurt profits and cause the company to miss earnings expectations.

2. Management of the company is slightly quirky by Wall Street standards, as evidenced by their willingness to forsake near-term results.

3. Also, somewhat odd is their willingness to allow such a large cash balance to build up over the past two years. Although we hope that management will use this cash to increase shareholder value, through either a dividend increase or stock buy-back, there is the chance that management could use this money for an ill-advised acquisition of another company or business, or use the money to rapidly open new Costco

stores in the United States or expand internationally. Such an expansion of the business could prove risky and could overwhelm management.

4. Lastly, with the stock currently around $45 per share, the stock sells for 24 times trailing earnings, which is fairly expensive for a retail company. With the valuation so rich, any significant disappointment by the company in terms of sales and earnings growth could cause the stock to drop sharply.

What Is The Stock Worth? Valuation And Setting A Price Target

Now that we have outlined the company's positive and negative attributes, the most critical task is to determine what Costco stock is worth, and based on this expected price target, determine if the stock is a buy, a sell, or something in between (a "hold" in Wall Street parlance).

The Price Earnings (P/E) Ratio

The most useful way to value Costco is to determine a target price for the company's stock based on the company's earnings and free cash flow. With Costco's stock at $45 per share and the company's earnings per share in 2004 of $1.85 per share, the stock's P/E ratio is 24.3 ($45 divided by $1.85 = 24.3). This P/E ratio is known as the "trailing" P/E ratio since it is based on the prior, or trailing twelve months earnings.

Investors also look at estimated forward P/E ratios, which are based on what investors and analysts expect the company to earn in the twelve months ahead. We will discuss this forward ratio for Costco shortly. Looking at the trailing P/E ratio of 24.3, it seems high when compared to the average stock in the market. Using the S&P 500 Index as an average, or norm, (the S&P 500 is an Index comprised of roughly the 500 largest public companies in the United States), we can find out that the average stock in the S&P 500 Index sells at 19.1 times trailing earnings. The average company in the S&P 500 Index saw earnings per share increase 7-8% from 2003 to 2004. Costco's earnings increase of 22 percent in 2004 was far better than the average company in the S&P 500. Unless we believe that this 22 percent increase was a one-time event, Costco should be valued more highly and therefore trade at a higher P/E ratio than the average company in the S&P 500 Index. I believe that Costco's earnings will continue to increase at an above average rate and should trade at a premium P/E multiple to the S&P Index. The issue then is what is a fair P/E multiple for Costco's present and future earnings.

Before we arrive at what the appropriate P/E ratio for Costco is, it would be helpful to look at the P/E ratio for other investments. Let's start with companies that are very similar to Costco, namely other large, growing retail companies. By doing some digging, we can find that Wal-Mart is selling for 20.3 times 2004 earnings per share and Target Corp is selling for 27.7 times 2004 earnings per share. Given the similarities between all these companies, we see that Costco's trailing P/E ratio of 24.3 is not out of line with the group. Some retailers that are growing at very rapid rates such as Starbucks or Whole Foods Markets, sell for more than 40 times their trailing earnings per share. Slow growth retailers such as JC Penny or Safeway sell for less than 20 times trailing earnings per share.

None of these comparisons tells us what is the appropriate P/E ratio for Costco. Perhaps investors are foolishly paying too much for Target stock. If they are, then perhaps Costco is also too expensive. An analogy here can once again be made to real estate. Most real estate prices are based on what similar properties in the same neighborhood recently sold for. If I have a 3,000 square-foot house on one-half an acre and a neighboring house with similar dimensions recently sold for $200,000, it is likely that my own property is worth somewhere close to that. Perhaps my home has certain items such as a new kitchen or a finished basement that make it more valuable, but essentially, its value will not be that different from the house nearby that was recently sold. With this logic, it is often helpful to look at companies similar to the one we are examining, to get a rough idea of what investors are willing pay in terms of a price multiple for a company's earnings per share. Once we have done that, it is then useful to differentiate the company we are examining from the average company in the industry and determine whether this differentiation warrants a discount or premium valuation to the "average" company in the industry.

It is also useful to see what P/E ratio investors are willing to pay for asset types other than stocks. For example, it is possible to look at bonds and see what P/E multiple is associated with fixed income investments. Looking at the business section of the newspaper, we can find that ten year U.S. Government bonds are yielding 4.25%. How do we calculate a P/E ratio for these bonds? Simple. Investors who purchase $100 of these bonds will earn $4.25 for holding these bonds for a full year. In effect, investors are paying 23.5 time earnings for these bonds ($100 divided by $4.25 = 23.5).

How does this P/E ratio relate to what should be a reasonable P/E ratio (earnings multiple) for Costco? Investors will pay a high P/E for government bonds because they are very safe investments and will return the promised yield (earnings) under nearly all circumstances. On the downside, however, the yield (or earnings) will never increase. It will pay the exact same income amount until it matures. Costco's earnings are not nearly as safe and secure as the income from a U.S. Treasury bond. However, Costco's earnings are very likely to increase meaningfully over time.

Setting the target using the P/E ratio

The question that the investor must ask is, "If investors in U.S. Government bonds are willing to pay 23.5 times earnings for an income stream that is very secure but not increasing at all, then what is a reasonable price to pay for earnings that are less secure but increasing at an annual rate of 20 percent?" Also, if investors are willing to pay in excess of 20 times earnings for other retail companies that may not have all the positive attributes that we were able to find in Costco (increasing earnings, no net debt, free cash flow, good management, etc), what is the "right" P/E ratio for Costco? With all the information we have, it is easy to argue that Costco should sell for 25 times earnings.

But what is this earnings amount? Costco earned $1.85 per share in 2004 and based on business trends, earnings should increase an additional 20 percent in 2005, resulting in 2005 earnings per share of approximately $2.20. It therefore seems reasonable that as current year 2005 earnings unfold, the shares should sell for 25 times the coming year earnings estimate of approximately $2.20, resulting in the stock eventually reaching $55 per share. Fifty-five dollars per share would therefore seem to be a reasonable price target for Costco stock, using earnings per share as a basis for valuing the stock.

Using Free Cash Flow As A Measure To Value Costco Stock

Is there another way to value to Costco besides using earnings per share? In our analysis of Costco, we have spent time discussing Costco's substantial free cash flow and how it can be used to benefit investors. Often, a company's stock price will be determined by its free cash flow rather than its earnings.

Many investors regard free cash flow as more important than earnings because the cash flow represents money that can be distributed to investors, whereas earnings may be accounting gimmickry and not "true" cash. Recall that in 2004, Costco was able to produce $1.4 billion of free cash flow after generating $700 million of free cash flow in 2003. As Costco has 480 million shares outstanding, this free cash equals $2.92 in free cash flow per share in

2004 and $1.46 per share in 2003. The free cash flow yield *(the free cash flow per share divided by the share price)* was 6.5% in 2004 and nearly 3.5% in 2003.

As we can see, the total free cash flow, free cash flow per share, and the free cash flow yield are all increasing rapidly. Refer back to the cash flow of the ten-year U.S. Treasury bond mentioned earlier. It yields 4.25% and its yield is not growing, but the receipt of the payment year after year is guaranteed. Costco's free cash yield is nearly 1.5 times the yield of the government bond and its yield is actually increasing every year. If current trends continue, Costco's free cash flow yield could be in excess of ten percent within just a few years. Given the growth in Costco's fee cash yield, the current yield of 6.5% relative to the non-growing Treasury bond's yield of 4.25% seems too low. It might be more reasonable for Costco's free cash flow yield to only be 5% since it is increasing from one year to the next. How does the yield go from 6.5% to 5%? The share price must go higher. How high? Since the company's $1.4 billion of free cash flow in 2004 resulted in a 6.5% yield on a market capitalization (total company size) of $21.6 billion, a 5% yield will result if the market capitalization increases to $28 billion ($1.4 billion divided by 5%, or .05 equals $28 billion). With a total market value of $28 billion and 480 million shares outstanding, each share should then sell for just over $58 per share ($28 billion divided by 480 million equals $58.33*). Please note that this is not an easy concept to grasp on the first reading. Please read the above several times if necessary, or continue on in this book and try to return to this section when you are more comfortable and confident.*

Let's reflect for a minute on our valuation analysis. Using a price to earnings multiple of 25 times 2005 estimated earnings, we arrive at a price target of $55 per share. Using a free cash flow yield target of 5%, we arrive at a price target of $58 per share. As potential investors, it is now fair to say that we expect Costco to trade to this mid to high-fifties level within the next twelve months. **This is our price target.** With the stock price currently trading around $45 per share, our target prices represents a potential gain of 22%–29% if Costco's stock price reaches our target range. This would be a very good one-year return on our investment.

Downside Risk

Lastly, we need to attempt to quantify our downside risk. Anytime an investor purchases a stock, he or she must realize that any investment in the stock market can result in a substantial loss, particularly when the stock purchased is risky and speculative.

With healthy companies such as Costco, absent fraud or criminal acts by management, the company is very unlikely to go bankrupt and the stock should maintain some level of value, even if the business goes through difficult times. What we try to do is establish a floor price for Costco's stock, a level through which the stock is unlikely to break, even if the company experiences short-term problems. To estimate a floor for Costco, we look at the company's 2004 earnings and assume that with the business expanding, there is very little chance that earnings in 2005 will be lower than 2004. However, if the economy weakens or the company does not execute it's business plan well, it is possible that earnings might only be up 10 percent instead of the company's more typical 20 percent or greater. If earnings are up only 10 percent in 2005, they would reach $2.04 per share ($1.85 x 1.10). Investors would be disappointed by this slower earnings growth, They may no longer be willing to pay 24 times earnings for the stock. Assuming, that after this earnings disappointment, they are only willing to pay a price of 19 times earnings for Costco, the stock would fall to 19 times $2.02, or just over $38 per share, down seven dollars from the current share price. A loss of 7 dollars in the share price of Costco would represent a decline of nearly 16 percent.

The free cash flow that Costco generates should act as a floor on Costco's stock. Even if earnings do not increase significantly in the coming years, free cash flow should remain very strong. If the stock were to decline, management can use some of the huge cash horde to buy back stock and/or increase the dividend. It is unlikely that the shares could get much below $38, given the huge amount of cash available to shareholders.

Risk/Reward Conclusion

Based on our analysis of Costco's business and methods of valuing that business, it is reasonable to conclude that Costco's stock, currently selling for around $45 per share is likely to be worth $55-58 per share after one year. This would represent a return on our investment of 22-29%. However, if Costco falters and its stock falls to 38, which seems like a reasonable floor, we would lose 16% of our investment. From a risk/reward standpoint, this seems like a very favorable situation.

As investors, we will almost never find a situation offering upside potential without some measure of risk. Our goal is to find investments that, after a thorough analysis, appear to have a favorable risk/reward profile—more upside potential than downside risk. Analyses rooted in fundamentals and sound valuation techniques have kept me out of many bad situations and provide me the conviction to add to investments that I already own when the share price drops for no logical reason. You may find other methods that work for you, but I recommend that any method you use be rooted in a fundamental analysis of the business and what that business is reasonably worth using sound and conservative valuation estimates and techniques.

Avoiding Bad Investments

How To Spot Red Flags In A Company's Financial Statements

Overstock.com

Having analyzed Costco's 2004 10-K and concluded that Costco is likely to be a solid investment, let's contrast that rosy picture with a company whose 10-K and Proxy Statement present more than a few red warning flags to investors. There are many dismal potential investments out there; in fact there are many outright scams and frauds.

I have selected a company, Overstock.com *(ticker symbol OSTK)*, that appears to have a few significant risks. Overstock.com does not appear to be a scam or fraud, but the company's SEC filings are riddled with information that should cause an investor to seriously question whether an investment in the company is a wise decision. I will highlight the red flags in the order that they appear in the 10-K and the Proxy Statement. I will not devote the same level of detailed analysis that we undertook with Costco. I simply want to give investors examples of various warning signs. Before we go through this analysis, let me state that I have no knowledge that Overstock.com is anything less than a relatively new company trying to grow its Internet retail business. I have no grudge with the company or management and I have no short position in the stock or options. I would be happy to see them succeed and disprove my skepticism. However, in reading through their 10-K and Proxy Statement, I found numerous items of concern that prevent me from investing in the company.

Flaws In The Business Plan

Let's look at Overstock.com's 2004 10-K, which can be found at http://www.sec.gov/Archives/edgar/data/1130713/000104746905006713/a21537

15z10-k.htm, and highlight what might make this company's stock a disappointing investment.

The company's business description, an "online 'closeout' retailer," would place it in a very crowded field where several larger, well-established companies" such as Amazon and EBay dominate due to their name recognition and "first on the scene" advantage. Other companies such as Barnes & Noble and Circuit City are able to sell retail items profitably on-line but that is because they already have a successful bricks and mortar business and the name recognition that goes along with it. Overstock.com would appear to be a new entrant with tremendous barriers to overcome to get potential customers to visit its website. In addition, the 10-K states that the company began an auction site that would seem to be a competitor with EBay. EBay is clearly the king of the internet auctions and even internet behemoths, such as Yahoo!, have failed to challenge EBay's dominance of online auctions. How likely is it that a new company, with no unique competitive advantage, can profitably challenge EBay? Sounds like a long shot. Lastly, on page three, the company states that in January of 2005, Overstock reopened its online travel store, offering cruise trips and other travel services. Retail closeouts, auctions, travel services.... for a relatively small company with a limited operating history, Overstock.com seems to be unfocused.

Skipping ahead to page 12 of the 10-K, we see a list of risk factors related to Overstock.com's business. "We have a history of significant losses." This certainly is not good, but not necessarily fatal if the company's business is growing and the losses are narrowing. We will see if this is the case with Overstock.com. On page 13, the company states that they will, "continue to incur significant operating expenses and capital expenditures." This does not give much comfort to investors expecting the business to turn profitable. Reading through the remaining risk factors, we see other statements that do not sound promising—"on-line retailers such as Amazon.com, Inc, Buy.com, Inc. and EBay, Inc have discount departments." "Substantially all of our computer and communications hardware is located a single facility in Salt Lake City." That sounds risky. What if there is a technical problem at that one site? Does this mean that the company will soon be spending large amounts of cash to build a second, back-up facility? What does having only one site say about management's prudence and planning? Looking ahead to page 21—"We have significant indebtedness." When we look at the company's balance sheet, we will try to determine how risky is the company's debt level. Lastly, on page 28, under the heading of, "Legal Proceedings", it appears that the company is being sued for allegedly selling counterfeit products on its website.

Weaknesses In The Financial Statements

Turning to page 31 of Overstock's 2004 10-K, we see the first set of financial data that the company provides. Simply by doing some basic, common sense calculations, we can see that Overstock is not on any fast track to profitability.

Notice that sales from 2000 to 2001 increased approximately 50 percent. Sales increased a further 119 percent in 2002 but only 75 percent in 2003 and sales growth slowed to 54 percent in 2004. While a 54 percent sales gain is certainly impressive, the rate of growth is decelerating, which for a company this small and young is disappointing. More disappointing is that while the rate of sales growth is slowing, the increase in the rate of operating expense growth is rising. Note that sales and marketing expenses and general and administrative expenses nearly doubled in 2004 (up 100%), the same year that sales increased by only 54 percent. (Skipping ahead to page 35 we see the company's mention of "customer acquisition cost"[4] increasing from $12.09 in 2003 to $16.43 in 2004. This is a very bad trend. Overstock needs to spend more and more on advertising to acquire each new customer. It will be very difficult for the company to ever become profitable if this trend continues.)

What investors should look for is a business with leverage to the bottom line—that is, sales are increasing faster than expenses. Most good businesses succeed with this principle. A store that sells ten percent more items from one year to the next, does not also need to spend ten percent more on rent, insurance, salaries, etc to achieve those sales gains. That is how even slow-growing businesses can achieve double-digit profit growth from one year to the next while only increasing sales by perhaps 3 to 6 percent. Overstock.com appears to be doing just the opposite. Not a good thing. This is evident on the bottom line—profits. We see that losses began to narrow in 2002 only to widen significantly in 2003. There is no steady course to profitability here.

On page 45, we see that over the past several years, Overstock.com raised significant amounts of cash by selling stock to the public in an initial public offering and through additional stock sales following its IPO. Notice that the company also sold $113 million of convertible notes in 2004. Convertible notes are a form of debt. These borrowings increase the company's expenses by adding additional interest to its list of required payments. In addition, the debt must be repaid when it comes due in 2011, increasing the risk that the company may fail. The stock and debt issuances are an indication that the company

---

4   *Customer acquisition costs are what a business spends, on average, to acquire a single new customer. These expenses are primarily comprised of advertising, marketing, and incentives such as rebates or discounts.*

is burning through cash. Now let's go to page F-6 of the 10-K and see if this is in fact the case.

The Statement Of Cash Flows—Some Red Flags

When we look at the Statement of Cash Flows on page F-6, we see that 2003 was a pretty bad year in terms of positive cash flow. Overstock lost more than ten million dollars from operations even before spending on additions to property and equipment. 2004 looks to be better with $25 million of cash flow from operations, but let's see if this is really the case.

Looking at the segment, "Cash Flows from Operating Activities", we see that net income for the year was a loss of $5 million. The adjustments to net income to arrive at cash flow can show if a company is manipulating items to make cash flow look better than it really is. The two easiest items for a company to play around with are accounts receivable (money that the company takes in from customers) and accounts payable (money that a company pays out to its suppliers). We see that the change in accounts receivable added nearly $4.5 million ($4.468) to cash flow from operations. What most likely happened here is that Overstock stepped up its efforts to collect cash from customers and the total amount the company was owed by its customers went down by $4.5 million from 2003 to 2004. Certainly not a bad thing, but the increase in cash did not come from increased sales, it just came from taking in money that was already owed to the company. It is a bit like finding loose change under your sofa cushions. Sure, it is cash coming in, but it is most likely a one-time event and while your cash inflow for the year is up, it is not at all due to business being healthier.

The next item we want to examine is the accounts payables balance. Now this looks a little scary. What we see here is that accounts payable, what the company owes its suppliers, went up by $33.7 million ($33.697) from 2003 to 2004. What this indicates to us is that Overstock.com owes $33.7 million more to its suppliers at the end of 2004 than it did at the end of 2003. Essentially, the company took in goods (inventory), and perhaps sold them, but did not pay for them yet. The company may have sold these items and reported them as a cash inflow, but has yet to pay for them and record the outflow. However, unless the company plans on stiffing its suppliers, these are payments that must be made in 2005 or its suppliers will cut Overstock.com off and eventually force it out of business.

The analogy I can make here to our personal finances is that if we were to not pay our landlord rent for the last six months of 2004, our cash flow would look great (cash from salary comes in, but no payments go out for rent). However, we would simply be borrowing from the future, as at some point we must either pay our landlord or he will kick us out. That is essentially what Overstock.com has done here. It would appear that they have delayed paying their suppliers to the tune of $33.7 to make their cash balances look higher than they would be if they were to pay their bills on time. In fact, were the company to pay its bills on time and have no increase in accounts payable from 2003 to 2004, cash flows from operations would have once again been negative (to the tune of nearly $9 million) in 2004 before the company even spent money on capital expenditures for new property and equipment. Definitely an ugly cash flow statement.

Other Items

There are other items in Overstock.com's 10-K that should strike the reader as odd or troublesome. Turning a few pages forward to F-29 of the 10-K, there is the mention of Overstock.com lending up to $10 million to "an entity for the purpose of buying inventory." It further states that Overstock has already loaned the entity $8.4 million at an interest rate of 3.75%. This seems very odd. Why can't Overstock simply purchase the inventory itself? Why loan money to some unknown entity at the amazingly low rate of 3.75%? It would seem that there is not even any collateral or security for this loan. I would love to borrow money for myself at 3.75% but the lowest rate I can find is around 6% and that is only if I use the money to buy a house and use the house as collateral to secure the loan. If I borrow money to buy a car, the bank will charge 8% and has the car as collateral. If I want to borrow money from my credit card company to buy useless junk, the rate is 18%.

So why is Overstock.com willing to lend money at 3.75% and who is this unknown "entity"? No details are given, but perhaps the entity is run by someone related to the CEO of Overstock and this is a way of setting them up in a profitable venture. I am not saying this is the case, but the favorable terms being given to this entity and the lack of explanation for it make us wonder (and so should you as the reader of the 10-K and potential investor—just use common sense, ask yourself, "Does this sound right? If it doesn't, it may be a warning to stay away from this company's stock!).

Management And The Board Of Directors—You're Gonna Trust This Crew With Your Money???

The icing on the cake for what makes Overstock.com look like a dicey bet can be found in the company's Proxy Statement. If you noticed, Overstock's 10-K did not have a separate section highlighting management and the board of directors, as Costco did. You would think if management and the Board were a stellar bunch, they would want to bring attention to themselves and their accomplishments in the 10-K. They missed the opportunity, so we'll have to find them in the Proxy Statement, which can be found at: http://www.sec.gov/Archives/edgar/data/1130713/000104746905008043/a2154479zdef14a.htm.

The first director listed, who is also up for re-election, is Allison Abraham. Ms. Abraham is 42, which is young for a director of a public company, but perhaps her experience makes up for her relative youth. The Proxy states that she is currently a consultant to several early stage technology companies. That doesn't really tell us anything. What is her past career experience? Ms. Abraham was chief operating officer of iVillage, an online media company from May, 1998–May, 2000. Not mentioned in the Proxy Statement is the fact that the company's share price went from 130 down to 9.50 while Ms. Abraham was COO. That's information most investors would like to know (and relatively easy to find with a simple Internet search). Before her term at iVillage, Ms. Abraham spent 14 months as chief operating officer of failed online grocer, Shopper's Express. I would be curious to find out what Overstock saw in this resume to ask her to be a director of the company.

Director number two, John Fischer, appears to have an impressive background.

The third director, Patrick Byrne, the company's CEO and a director, has held several CEO positions in the past, but I am not sure that he has been in any prior position that would prepare him to run an internet retail company. Also notice on the bottom of page 23 that Patrick Byrne also serves as the chairman and controls High Plains Investments, LLC which is Overstock's largest shareholder. This is a situation that could present conflicts with small shareholders (you, the reader). The Compensation Committee of the Board states that it does not believe this is the case, but look who is on the Board—should you place much weight in their opinion???

The fourth director is Patrick Byrne's father, John Byrne. The elder Byrne is the past chairman and CEO of White Mountain Insurance. Based on public filings of Mr. Byrne's holdings in White Mountain, he is a very wealthy man.

Investors should ask themselves if that wealth has enabled his son to become the CEO of the various companies he has headed. In other words, is Patrick Byrne the CEO because of his merit or because his father has backed him?

The fifth director is Gordon Macklin, who just so happens to be the current CEO of White Mountain Insurance.

This clearly is a board of directors whose relationship extends beyond the business of overseeing the affairs of the company. A board of five directors is very small to begin with, and of the five, three are clearly related to the CEO in some way. As for the 4th, it remains unclear how someone as unimpressive as Ms. Abraham got her spot, but she may know the Byrnes as well. Investors must be on the watch for a Board that has interests or relationships that may conflict with what is best for outside shareholders. Whenever you see a Board like this, it is my opinion that it is advisable to stay away. Read the 10-K, read the Proxy Statement. Don't find out about potential conflicts from a newspaper article, after you have lost most of your investment.

Lastly, look at the management of the company, listed on page 24. The ages of the all the top officers should hit any potential investor like a sledgehammer on the head. This group is most likely not experienced enough to run a public company. Maybe one or two of these individuals possess enough brilliance to offset their lack of experience, but it is very doubtful that all of them do. Finally, notice that Mr. Byrne and his family and other related entities control this company through their majority ownership. They may cause the company to enter into transactions that harm small, outside shareholders, but benefit themselves.

Please use this company as a guide for what to avoid when seeking out good investments. I have nothing against Overstock.com or its CEO. I hope they succeed, but it would be wiser to watch from the sidelines, than to invest in the company.

Stock Value Derived From Corporate Assets

We've examined Costco, which seemed to be a pretty good investment candidate and we've contrasted that company with Overstock.com, an investment that seems more than a little risky. Next we will examine a company that doesn't necessarily have growing earnings, free cash flow or talented management or tons of cash or any of the attributes that made Costco so attractive. Can such a company be a good investment? Perhaps.

Let's look at a situation where a stock may be a good investment as a result of the assets that it owns, rather than the earnings or cash flow that it generates. Whereas Costco derived its value from its earnings and cash flow stream, asset-rich companies derive their value from the assets they own or control. The downside to investing in asset-value companies is that is often difficult to realize the value of these assets without some event taking place, such as a takeover or sale of the company. Such an event sometimes does not occur because the management that controls the company does not want the sale or takeover to take place because such a transaction would cost them their well-paying jobs if it were to be completed.

There are many companies whose share price is not based on what the company is earning or generating in free cash flow. Instead, the share price is based on the value of the assets that the company owns, that investors hope will one day be converted into cash. For example, an oil exploration company may spend years of time and millions of dollars drilling for oil. For its efforts, the company may only have huge losses to show. But, if after several years, the company is able to locate a significant reservoir of oil, the value of the company and its share price should be very high. Why should the company have any value if it reports losses year after year and may not have earnings for several more years until the oil can be extracted? As should be obvious, the company has value because it has assets that one day will be sold for a large gain. The oil in the ground has a value even though it has not yet been converted to cash. As investors, we expect that in the foreseeable future, the oil will be produced and sold and the resulting cash will benefit investors.

Maui Land & Pineapple Company, Inc.

A company that we will examine as an example of a firm with little or no earnings but tremendous potential asset value is Maui Land & Pineapple (*ticker symbol MLP; website mauiland.com*).

Maui Land & Pineapple is a company formed in the 1930's to grow pineapple and other crops, on land amassed on the island of Maui, Hawaii. For the past seventy years, the company has sold pineapples grown on its Maui property. The pineapple business has been marginally profitable. However, in the past three years, the price of MLP stock has more than doubled from 15 to its current trading range of 30 to 40. At the current price of 31, Maui Land has a market capitalization of just under $230 million (7.2 million shares outstanding x $31 = $223.2 million).

Why are investors buying the stock when the company's profits were relatively small in 2003 and were negative in 2004? The answer is best explained by the company's decision several years ago to develop some of the vast parcels of land that MLP owns in Maui. Some investors are speculating that as MLP develops and sells parcels of its property, it will be able to earn far more money from its real estate holdings than it can from selling pineapples. Take a look at MLP's 2004 10-K and see what possible value MLP might have. Maui Land and Pineapple's 2004 10-K can be found at: http://www.sec.gov/Archives/edgar/data/63330/000104746905008076/a2153751z10-k.htm

The Assets

Page one of Maui Land's 10-K describes the company's various business segments. We see that the company's businesses encompass pineapple farming, resort operations on the company's property, development of the company's real estate, and an interest in a retail mall that has since been sold. It is worth a read to understand the operations of the pineapple business, but that is not the basis of our interest in the company.

We are concerned with the potential value of the company's substantial property holdings. Page six of the 10-K describes the company's vast land holdings in Maui. According to the company's filing, Maui Land & Pineapple owns 28,600 acres of land in Maui which was acquired between 1911 and 1932. Of this land, the company has essentially donated 13 acres in Kapalua to the state of Hawaii and donated an additional 8,600 acres to The Nature Conservancy of Hawaii (technically MLP has not donated this land but has granted a permanent easement to the state of Hawaii and The Nature Conservancy, which prevents MLP from developing the land in perpetuity.) Without these two parcels, Maui Land still owns and controls just under 20,000 acres on the island. The company describes this land as including nine miles of oceanfront acreage and elevated property that rises from the ocean to a height of 5,700 feet. In addition to the raw land, MLP owns the resort buildings and improvements which include three golf courses, a ten court tennis facility, a 22,00 square foot shopping center, over 700 residential lots, homes and water and sewer lines that service the property.

Estimating The Value Of The Assets

Trying to determine the value of this property is somewhat imprecise. The company's 10-K provides little clue about what the land and improvements might be worth.

On page 34, the balance sheet lists the company's assets and shows the land, improvements, and buildings having a stated value of nearly $110 million.

However, investors should be aware that assets listed on a company's balance sheet are typically valued at cost. In fact, on page 38, the company explicitly states that land value is carried at cost. Bear in mind that the company's 28,600 acres were purchased between 1911 and 1932. Chances are, Hawaiian real estate cost a lot less seventy-five years ago than it is worth today. If the Dutch still owned Manhattan, their balance sheet would still show the value as being $24.

We might want to ask, "How is the stock market valuing MLP's land and other assets?" The stock market valuation of the entire Maui Land & Pineapple company is approximately $230 million (7.2 million shares x $31 per share). The company has a negligible amount of debt and nearly as much cash in the bank as it does debt so essentially there is no mortgage on the property and MLP owns everything outright. Essentially, the stock market is valuing each acre of MLP's land at approximately $11,500 per acre ($230,000,000 divided by 20,000 acres). It is important to remember that not every acre of Maui Land's property can be developed and sold. Generally, environmental restrictions, zoning laws, and community opposition can severely limit the amount of real estate that a large landowner can develop or sell. Even assuming that only 1/3 of MLP's acreage can eventually be developed, the land is still valued at only $35,000 per acre. This may be an expensive price for farmland in the interior of the United States, however, for coastal property in Hawaii, it seems tremendously undervalued.

Other than the risks mentioned above (possible restrictions on MLP's ability to develop much of the property), there are other significant risks related to an investment in Maui Land. For starters, if the company is poorly managed, MLP may spend far more in developing the property than they will be able to recoup from the eventual sales of home sites and homes. MLP might be best served selling the land in its undeveloped state to buyers who wish to build their own residences. As we see in the 10-K, however, MLP is developing the property in the hopes that it can make a larger profit selling the finished product as opposed to just the raw land. Should MLP not manage the construction properly, and cost overruns ensue, any houses sold may be sold at a loss.

Certainly, there are other risks as well, some of which can never be predicted by investors—boxers will tell you that the punch that knocked them out is the one they never saw. In Maui Land's case, that punch could be land contamination from pesticides previously used in farming, perhaps a long-dormant volcano nearby blows its top and covers MLP's 28,600 acres in lava. One never knows. However, if MLP is able to develop and sell its land holdings for anything close to the current market value of real estate in Maui, the value of the land could be worth well in excess of one billion dollars.[5] Any calculation of land value or speculation on what could go wrong leaves room for an incredibly wide range of values for what Maui Land & Pineapple stock is worth.

The important point to take away from this exercise, however, is to realize that the value of a company's stock may be determined by items other than its earnings or cash flow. Often, as in the case of MLP, the company's ownership of certain assets such as real estate or valuable patents, or breakthrough drugs in development (note that most biotech companies do not have any earnings, yet the shares often increase sharply on news that a company is working on a new drug) may determine the price of that company's stock.

Having examined the financial statements of Costco, Overstock.com, and Maui Land & Pineapple, you should have a good idea of what I look for when deciding whether or not to purchase the shares of a particular company. While no two people have the exact same approach to investing, my hope is that readers of this book have learned a few fundamentals upon which to base their investment decisions. Investing is part science and part art, and as a result, no simple formula can be used to determine whether or not a stock is good investment. Besides, if it were possible to find good investments by using a formula, everyone with a calculator would be rich. My goal is for you to at least add some of your intuition and skill to some of my formulas and thought processes.

---

5   *Assume the land is worth, on average, $100,000 per acre (oceanfront land worth over $1 million per acre, unusable land worth $25,000 per acre, and other parcels somewhere in between)—$100,000 per acre x 20,000 acres = $2 billion—If the value of the land, and in turn, the company, is worth $2 billion, each share of MLP would sell for over $270! ($2 billion divided by 7.2 million shares = 278.*

PART II

Learning About Various Industries

Most investors do not need to have an in-depth knowledge of all the various industries that are available for possible investment. It is sufficient to simply be familiar with several that you find interesting or believe will do well in the years to come. Even in my capacity as a mutual fund manager, I do not have an intimate understanding of all the different industries that exist. There are simply too many industries and companies for one person to follow. I am not an expert in technology companies, but this deficiency is dwarfed by the areas in which I do have a great deal of knowledge.

For individual investors, I recommend finding a few areas of interest. Start with industries that are relatively easy to understand such as retailers or personal products companies such as Proctor & Gamble and Colgate. It can also be fun to research industries that interest you. If you have an interest in science or medicine, try to learn more about the pharmaceutical, biotechnology, and medical device industries and the companies within them.

It is possible to learn a great deal about a particular industry by reading the Business Description section of the 10-K of a company that operates in that industry. Want to learn about the energy business? Read the Business Description section in ExxonMobil's 10-K. Biotechnology companies provide detailed descriptions of the drugs they have in development and their research processes. With the Internet and search engines, it is possible to go to Askjeeves.com or Google and simply type in a question such as, "How can I learn more about the railroad industry?" and come up with lots of useful information. For even more information and knowledge, I recommend purchasing textbooks that go into great detail about particular businesses and industries.

Growth Industries Vs. Cyclical Industries

It is important that investors know the two broadest company and industry classifications. Generally, most businesses can either be classified as growth or cyclical businesses. **Growth stocks** are stocks of companies whose sales consistently increase from one year to the next, regardless of the economic environment. Typical growth industries are pharmaceutical and biotechnology companies, supermarkets, hospitals, utilities, medical device manufacturers, communication and media companies, food and beverage companies.

A growth company can be healthcare-related, such as a hospital, a pharmaceutical manufacturer, or a medical device manufacturer. These companies usually see sales and profits increase steadily from one year to the next. That is not to say that sales and profits do not ever fall from one year to the next. However, when sales or profits do fall, it is usually the result of a company-specific problem such as a product recall (Merck & Co.'s Vioxx) or competition from a rival and not due to general economic weakness.

Because growth stocks are capable of earning increased profits consistently year after year, they are often favored by investors and sell for high price-earnings ratios. A good-quality growth company will often sell for 20-25 times earnings and it is not unusual to see rapidly growing companies selling for 35-50 times earnings. The risk of owning stocks with such high price—earnings ratios is that if the company stumbles and earnings do not increase as rapidly as investors had anticipated, the drop in share price can be dramatic. If investors decide that rather than selling at 40 times earnings, a stock is more appropriately valued at 20 times earnings, the share price will drop by 50 percent. Ouch.

Cyclical stocks are stocks of those companies whose fate is tied to the direction of the economy. The fortunes of these companies run in *cycles,* hence the term cyclical. When the economy is strong, these companies usually report increases in revenue and huge increases in profits from one year to the next. When the economy is slow or contracting, profits for these companies usually plummet and sometimes disappear altogether.

The most common types of cyclical companies are industrial-type concerns such as the auto manufacturers, heavy equipment suppliers, such as Deere and Caterpillar, and steel companies such as U.S. Steel and Nucor. Almost all manufacturing, mining, airline, and energy companies are considered cyclical. Their profits may not be exactly tied to the broader economic cycle, but they almost always experience sharp rises and drops in profits that correspond either to the economic cycle or to a boom and bust cycle that affects their particular business.

With these companies, it is usually best to buy them after they have fallen on hard times. Stocks tend to reflect expectations of future events. What this means, is that when cyclical companies are going through very good times, the stocks tend to go up at the beginning of the good times but stagnate or go down when the good times get even better. Why does this happen? Investors are assuming that revenue and profits are so good for these companies that the party will end soon.

It is important to remember that these are not growth companies; at some point the party will end. Investors anticipate this and want to be out of them before the cycle turns and profits disappear. Therefore, they sell when they feel that profits are about to peak. The mirror image tends to be true on the downside. The stocks will bottom when times are bad but will begin to rise even though a recovery is still not at hand. When times are bad, investors will eventually come to believe that a recovery is in the not too distant future and want to be on board to participate in the recovery.

Please note that some companies are not pure growth or pure cyclical companies. A retailer with a hot concept may rapidly open stores and increase sales and earnings for ten consecutive years. It is a growth stock but the overall industry of retailing is a cyclical business. Retail sales rise when the economy is healthy and can fall during periods of economic recession.

Value Stocks are stocks of companies that sell at very low price to earnings or price to free cash flow multiples. Value stocks can be stocks of either growth or cyclical companies. However, since growth companies typically sell at high price to earnings ratios and high price to free cash ratios, most value stocks are generally stocks of cyclical companies. Often, value stocks are stocks of companies that are out of favor for one reason or another.

At the moment, a good example of a value stock would be shares of grocery store companies such as Kroger, Safeway, and Albertson's. While the average stock in the S&P 500 sells for 19 times earnings, these companies sell for 14 times earnings. While that may not appear to be that steep of a discount to the average stock, it is important to remember that grocery stores are considered growth companies that are relatively immune to the ups and downs of the economy. These companies usually sold for a premium to the average stock. Often they would sell for 18-22 times earnings, since investors could count on their steady business and annual increases in earnings, cash flow, and dividends.

The shares of the grocery store companies fell into the Value bargain box after they disclosed that earnings were being hurt by the encroachment of Wal-Mart onto their supermarket turf. Several years ago, Wal-Mart began to aggressively open stores that sold food items at a discount to the traditional grocery stores. The supermarket companies have been forced to lower their prices to meet this challenge. As a result, earnings growth actually turned negative and earnings began to decrease from one year to the next. At the current time, some investors believe that these stocks are now cheap. They believe that although Wal-Mart is a threat, the supermarket companies will find ways to distinguish themselves from the behemoth retailer, either through superior product selection or superior service, and no longer be forced to compete simply on price. If that occurs, investors will once again treat these stocks as growth companies and perhaps value them at 16-20 times earnings, which will cause the share prices of these companies to increase significantly.

Pessimists, however, believe that the supermarket companies are "value traps"—they may look cheap but are actually companies in continuing decline, as the challenge from Wal-Mart will only grow as the giant retailer opens increasing numbers of superstores that sell grocery items. In addition, higher-end retailers such as Whole Foods Markets capture affluent food shoppers with offerings of organic produce and a higher level of service. As earnings continue to decline, these stocks will no longer appear cheap. Whether the optimists or skeptics are correct will only be determined by the passage of time. Finding treasures in the Value bin is a test of an investor's intuition and skill. What attracts the bargain hunters is the prospect of buying the ugly duckling value stock that turns into a swan.

Stocks Vs. Other Investments

As we discussed above, stocks are but one option investors have when looking to invest their savings. Although my experience and expertise lies primarily in equities (stocks), investors should have a balanced portfolio that includes bonds, cash, and real estate.

I have no set percentages that should be allocated to each type of investment and believe that the percentages should vary over time depending on which group offers the most upside based on risk/reward potential as well as the goals and needs of the individual investor. For example, a retiree with very little risk tolerance, should have a high percentage of his or her assets in cash and bonds to ensure a guaranteed current income. A young, employed couple with no children can safely undertake a higher degree of risk and should probably have a relatively high percentage of their assets in stocks or other asset types that involve the potential for large gain, but also the possible loss of principal.

Using The Price/Earnings Ratio To Evaluate Investments Other Than Stocks

To help determine which asset class (stocks, bonds, or real estate) is most attractive at any given time, investors need to look at the valuations of each group and use historical norms as a guide.

We have touched briefly on how Costco stock is valued versus ten-year Treasury bonds that yield 4.25%. We can use a similar analysis to compare stocks, bonds and other asset types such as real estate. The key metric to look at when comparing asset types is to look at the income that each asset produces and to look at every asset as having a price-earnings ratio that measures how cheap or expensive that asset is. As we discussed, a U.S. Treasury bond yielding 4.25% earns $4.25 for each $100 of bonds owned. The P/E ratio for this investment can be expressed as $100 divided by $4.25 or 23.5. This bond sells for 23.5 times its earnings.

Let's look at how we can examine real estate using a price to earnings measure. The following example is based on an actual ad for an apartment for sale that my wife asked me to examine to see if it looked like a good investment. The ad was for a 600 square foot apartment in Manhattan, occupied by a tenant. The tenant lives in the apartment with a one-year lease and pays rent of $1800 per month. The apartment price was listed at $499,000. Readers outside New York or California might reject this investment before doing any analysis, thinking that anyone who pays nearly $500,000 for a 600 square foot apartment should have their head examined. But, (unfortunately) homes and apartments in New York City are very costly, and perhaps this investment may appear reasonable after doing a financial analysis. Let's start by calculating the potential earnings for this investment (the "E" in the P/E ratio). Our tenant will pay $1,800 per month or $21,600 per year. As the landlord, we will have some expenses associated with the apartment. In New York City, apartment owners must pay common fees that cover real estate taxes, maintenance, and other costs related to the building (the doorman, super, etc). These costs tend to average about $1 per month per square foot. 600 square feet times $1 times 12 months = $7,200 per year. In addition, the owner of the apartment will also need to pay for heat, water, insurance, repairs, and other costs related to the apartment. These costs will probably average approximately $400 per month, or $4,800 per year. We may incur other unforeseen expenses or receive less income than expected if the tenant turns out to be a deadbeat, destructive, or decides to leave before the lease expires. However, assuming a best case scenario, our revenue from this tenant will be $21,600 and our expenses will be

$12,000 ($7,200 + $4,800), resulting in income of $9,600. The price of this investment is $499,000, the Price/Earnings ratio of this investment is 52 (*499,000 divided by 9,600*). Wow! That looks very high—far more expensive than U.S. Treasury Bonds, and with a lot more risk. We know that the government will pay us the interest due on the bonds. It is far less certain that our tenant in the above example will pay the rent.

Relationship Between P/E Ratio and Yield

Expressed another way we must invest $499,000 to earn, at most (remember, there is the chance our tenant does not pay or unexpected repairs are needed), $9,600 which equates to a yield of 1.92%. Compared to the ten-year Treasury bonds, which are risk-free and yield 4.25%, this looks like a pretty bad investment. (*Notice that the yield is the inverse of the price/earnings ratio of 52–1/52nd equals .0192, or 1.92%. It is important to remember this fact since every time you see a p/e ratio, you can do a quick calculation of the investment's current yield. For example, an investment with a p/e ratio of 15 has a yield of 1/15th, or 6.67%*)

Given the hot real estate market, it is likely that this apartment was sold at close to its $499,000 asking price. You might ask, why would someone purchase an apartment as an investment when its earnings yield is only 1.92%? (and that low yield also comes with some considerable risks) The answer is that in a hot market, whether it is for real estate, or stocks, or even bonds, investors take speculative risks and lose sight of the fundamentals. In New York, and other locales, apartments and condominiums are being sold where the rent revenue does not even meet the expenses of owning the property. The yield on the investment is actually negative.

What are these investors thinking? When asked, most of these investors state that they believe that after several years or less, they will be able to sell their investment for more than they paid. They believe that even though they are losing money while they own the property, the gain upon selling the property will more than offset the carrying loss. They believe that someone will want the privilege of owning an asset with negative cash flow for a price even higher than what they paid for it.

My belief is that these investors are in for a rude surprise and are falling victim to two of the classic investment mistakes—**the Bigger Fool Theory**, and, **Using the Past to Predict the Future.**

The Bigger Fool Theory

The Bigger Fool Theory states that investors will often buy assets, such as stocks or real estate, in rising markets because they believe that the markets will continue to rise, allowing them to sell their investment to a fool, even bigger than themselves, who will pay even more for the asset than they did.

In hot markets, this type of investing can work for short periods. However, like the game of musical chairs, eventually the music stops and things end badly. Eventually the market runs out of fools and if you are the last fool to buy, the investment is going to go down with you as the last, and biggest, fool.

The Fallacy Of Using The Past To Predict The Future

Using the past to predict the future is a mistake investors often make when deciding what to buy. Investors assume that what worked in the past will continue to work in the future. It is often said that generals plan for the previous war, and as a result are ill-prepared to fight the next battle, which is often completely different from the last one.

Every investment environment is different and the market leaders of the past are no more likely to be leaders tomorrow than any other investment idea. After the technology bubble burst in 2000, many investors were buying more technology stocks throughout their subsequent slide because they kept expecting the stocks to recover and bounce back. The NASDAQ stock index dropped from over 5,100 in March of 2000, to its low of 1,108 in October of 2002. All the way down, investors, convinced that technology stocks would rally again, threw money at the tech stocks in this Index. However, while technology stocks were being decimated, investments such as bonds and real estate were doing spectacularly well. Investors who kept open minds and were willing to look beyond technology stocks, at all their investment options, did well. Those who were myopic and continued to chase yesterday's winners, lost big.

What To Look For When Choosing Among Investment Options

One of the reasons I selected Costco as our sample 10-K to examine is that it contains so many of the positive attributes that I look for when I am trying to decide whether a company's stock will be a good investment. Just because Costco is blessed with all of these positive factors does not guarantee that Costco will be a winning stock. There are many things that can happen to derail an investment—management may unexpectedly leave the company, the company could be involved in some type of scandal, the demand for the company's products may decrease, competitors may become more aggressive, etc. However, having many of these positive attributes on your side, increases the odds that the investment will be a success. In addition, even if the investment does not work out, attributes such as a good management team, a debt-free balance sheet and free cash flow, help to ensure that any slide will be not be unduly severe.

Beyond The Financial Statements—What To Look For

In addition to the favorable data that we gleaned from Costco's 10-K and Proxy Statement, there are other attributes that investors should seek out when trying to find winning stock investments. Chief among these attributes is some type of "catalyst", which will propel the share price higher. Also important is some favorable macro trend that will act as a rising tide to lift all boats in the company's industry or area of operations.

Catalysts—A company may be the best business in the world but if no one knows about it, the stock is unlikely to move higher. That is a bit of an exaggeration of course, since there will always be a few investors, in addition to management, who are aware of the company's success. The thing to remember, though, is that it is it is important that there be some catalyst to get a stock price higher. That catalyst is some event or condition that will entice investors to buy shares of the company's stock, which will cause the share price to move higher. A catalyst can take many forms. A catalyst can be very specific, such as a company reporting higher sales and profits for a particular quarter or year, or very general, such as a growing interest in a particular industry, such as solar power, resulting from very high energy prices.

A real-life example of a broad, positive shift in opinion on a particular industry occurred in the energy industry this year. For most of the recent history of the energy industry, the price of petroleum was determined by how much supply the OPEC cartel was willing to sell into the market. There was a surplus of oil in the world but, because much of the supply was held by the OPEC bloc, they could artificially keep the price high by selling less than their full production capacity. In 1998, the price of oil collapsed to $10 per barrel, the result of OPEC supplying too much oil into the world market at the same time that an economic recession in Asia reduced demand for oil. The price collapse resulted in many oil companies canceling drilling projects. It was uneconomical to find and produce new sources of petroleum with the price so low.

Two years later, the price of oil recovered to $20 per barrel. Despite the price rise, most oil companies were reluctant to invest in new projects, fearing that the price might return to $10. As a result, very little new oil was discovered in the period of 1999 through 2004. Even OPEC was spending very little to expand their existing production capacity. In the meantime, the demand for oil was increasing. In 2004, demand increased significantly, as countries such as India and China industrialized at a frantic pace. In the United States, demand also rose sharply as consumers purchased record numbers of gas-guzzling SUV's and built ever-larger homes that consumed energy to heat them in the winter and cool them in the summer.

As an investor, I saw a huge catalyst in the confluence of all these events. It seemed obvious to me that energy prices would go higher. Very little investment was being undertaken by either OPEC or the major oil companies of the world, such as ExxonMobil, Chevron, or British Petroleum, to search for new energy in order to increase supply. At the same time, demand was rising sharply. In the past, OPEC could simply open the taps and produce more oil to meet the increased demand. But this time, demand had grown so much and OPEC had invested so little in new production, that OPEC was selling nearly 100 percent of its maximum potential output. As the price rose, I realized that this increase was different than in the past. With OPEC already producing nearly every barrel it could, the risk that OPEC would overproduce and send the price crashing back down was greatly diminished. Energy was in tight supply. OPEC and the oil companies of the world needed to spend more money to explore for and develop new oil reservoirs. The rising price of oil and the shortage of new oil were the catalysts for this increased spending. Suspecting this catalyst was coming, I found ways to participate in this more favorable outlook for the energy sector. I invested heavily in companies that made products that energy companies would need to find new energy. I bought the stocks of companies such as Transocean Offshore (RIG), Diamond Offshore (DO), and Pride International (PDE) that own drilling rigs that the oil companies hire to drill for oil and gas; I bought stocks in companies such as Schlumberger (SLB), Halliburton (HAL), and Grant Prideco (GRP), that sell drill bits, pipes and drilling fluids, all used in the drilling process. I also bought shares of companies that benefit from high oil and natural gas prices; stocks such as Chesapeake Energy, Amerada Hess, and Burlington Resources. These are all companies that drill for and sell oil and natural gas. With the price of these commodities at record levels, I expected that their profits would soar.

Of course, profiting from a potential catalyst is not as easy as simply reacting to the rise in the price of energy. You must predict these occurrences and act before they take place. The trick is to find the catalyst that will bring about the occurrence. For me, I saw that the energy companies had under-invested for many years in their efforts to find new energy. I believed that sooner or later this stinginess would catch up to the world by causing supply to be tight at the same time that demand was surging. There are many other catalysts that can be found that will lead to certain companies and industries being viewed more favorably by investors. With oil and gas prices so high, it would be reasonable to assume that the public would be more interested in alternative energy sources such as wind, solar and, hydro power. There are companies that derive all or a portion of their revenue and profits from these businesses. The trick is to find the catalyst before the majority of other investors do.

A catalyst does not necessarily have to be an event such as rise in the price of oil. A catalyst can be a financial condition, such as the accumulation of cash resulting from several years of excess free cash flow, that will cause a company's share price to rise. As smart investors, we know that a stockpile of cash can be used to increase the share price through dividend increases or significant share repurchases. By focusing on the Balance Sheet and Statement of Cash Flows, we can anticipate these catalysts before they actually occur, and buy the stock before the majority of the rest of the investing public is aware that good news is coming. When the good news arrives in the form of an announcement of a large dividend hike, we are there to participate in the stock moving higher.

Emerging Trends—Finding A Theme—Similar to the previous discussion of catalysts, investors can often be helped by choosing an investment in an industry that has favorable underlying trends. It is much easier to find profitable investments when you have the wind at your back as a result of an industry with favorable growth trends. These favorable trends can act as a catalyst when they develop and become more obvious to others. My discussion of the energy industry earlier can also be considered a general theme as much as it is a specific catalyst. There are many themes or trends that are taking place right now. I try to find broader, longer-lasting trends or themes. One of the trends I see right now is the increasing popularity of healthy eating among Americans. Despite the prevalence of obesity in the United States, there is a growing segment of the population that strives to eat healthier food. Beneficiaries of this trend are companies that sell or distribute organic produce. One of my largest investments is in the stock of the organic and naturals foods retailer, Whole Foods Markets (WFMI). The company is a rapidly growing retailer of natural and organic foods. The company's stores are large, well laid-out and offer a higher level of service than a traditional grocery store. As a result, the company is able to charge more and earn much higher profits than a traditional food retailer. On a price to earnings measure, the company's stock is not cheap and some critics claim that the company's growth will slow if customers become disenchanted with the store's high prices. My opinion, however, is that Whole Foods' prices are not that much higher than their competitors' and the superior shopping experience is worth the additional cost. Besides, consumers have shown that they are willing to pay a premium for a good or service that they perceive as superior—the success of Starbucks with its $3 cups of coffee, is testimony to this fact.

There are many other emerging trends that investors can capitalize on to find profitable investments. Investors may be exposed to these themes every day, but do not realize that they can use this knowledge and some financial smarts to profit from these themes. Several possible themes that you might consider when looking for favorable trends include the aging population in the United States, the increasing wealth of the American population, and the changing ethnic composition of the United States, most notably, the continuing increase of the Hispanic population in the U.S. To capitalize on the first trend, investors should consider companies that provide goods and services to the elder segment of the population. Beyond the usual businesses such as hospitals and pharmaceutical companies, investors might benefit from looking at companies that provide recreational activities such as travel aimed toward an older segment of the population. The theme of an aging population dovetails with our second theme above, which is the increased wealth of the American population. The reason these two themes are interrelated is that much of the wealth in the United States is concentrated in the hands of older Americans, who have achieved a measure of prosperity after many years of working and saving. In addition, much of this wealth is being transferred to their children either through inheritance or gifting. This increased wealth has led to a tremendous demand for luxury products that a generation ago might have only been attainable by a very small segment of society. Luxury is becoming more the norm, and it might be useful, from an investment standpoint, to find companies that cater to this increasingly wealthy segment. Beneficiaries of this trend would include luxury retailers such as Tiffany's, cruise providers such as Carnival and Royal Caribbean, auto makers BMW and Porsche, and upscale home builders, such as Toll Brothers.

The final trend I mentioned, the increasing size of the Hispanic population may be relatively limited in terms of public companies that benefit from it. However, there are several public companies, such as Univision Communications, that are direct beneficiaries of this trend. Investors may also try to seek out companies that are increasing their focus and attempts to market to Hispanic Americans. None of the broad themes mentioned above will lead straight to winning stocks. It is critical that you go through the financial analyses discussed previously in this book. It is also important that investors continue to use their common sense and good judgment whenever making any investment decision. The importance of spotting emerging themes and trends, however, is that it puts the wind at your back. I have long believed that it is better to invest in a poorly-run company operating in a very good industry than it is to invest in a well-run company operating in a dying industry. Your goal is to get as many variables as possible working in your favor—a good industry with favorable demographic trends, and a good company within that industry with good management and in solid financial condition. Given all these positive attributes, if the valuation is reasonable, the investment is likely to be a winner.

Socially responsible investing—Socially responsible investing, a relatively new phenomenon, is the practice of investing only in companies that produce some societal benefit, or at the very least, cause no harm. There are no set standards for what constitutes a socially responsible company, and as a result, socially responsible investing is not a well-defined topic. I will give you my take on socially responsible investing and how the concept guides my own investment decisions. My philosophy, when investing for my personal account, is to avoid companies that in some way harm society. However, as long as a company is not committing some act or product of harm, I am open to investing in it. Legally, the purpose of a corporation is to maximize profits for the shareholders. With profit maximization as its goal, it is no surprise that corporate managements often engage in behavior that does not comport with what is best for society as a whole. Furthermore, I believe that it is too restrictive to only invest in companies that better mankind. I do not believe that the purpose of a corporation is to benefit society. I believe that investors need to use their profits from investing and donate a portion of them to support charities or other organizations that do beneficial work such as scientific research, animal welfare, assistance to the poor, and environmental preservation.

It would also be somewhat arbitrary to favor companies that are "doing good" versus others that are simply trying to maximize profits. For example, Ben & Jerry's was often cited as a virtuous company because its CEOs were modestly paid and a portion of its profits were donated to charities. One could argue, however, that Ben & Jerry's products are extremely high in fat and contribute to the rampant obesity and heart disease in the United States. McDonald's, on the other hand, has been the subject of unflattering media reports because many of its offerings are high in saturated fat. A recent film, "Supersize Me", portrayed the company in a negative light. In addition, the company has even been named a defendant in several lawsuits claiming that McDonald's is responsible for the obesity of the plaintiffs. My take, is that McDonald's is selling a product that the public wishes to consume. Consumers are not being fooled or misled into purchasing the company's offerings. In addition, many of McDonald's new salads and non-beef entrees are fairly healthy and offer a good value to consumers who cannot afford full-service restaurants. In addition, the company performs a public service by allowing drivers `to use its bathrooms free of charge at its highway restaurants. I know this is a bit silly, but my point is that who is "virtuous" and who is "villainous" is far from clear-cut.

Furthermore, there are many companies and industries that are cast as unethical by some and well-regarded by others. I had always considered Johnson & Johnson to be a good model for most companies. The company has consistently increased earnings and dividends from one year to the next. In addition, the company has done a remarkable job of developing new medical and pharmaceutical products. The company is also known as a good place to work and is generally well-liked in the communities where it has offices and manufacturing plants. Interestingly enough, the company is on a list of stocks that should be avoided by certain religious institutions. Some of the company's surgical devices are used by physicians performing abortions and as a result, certain religious groups find the company objectionable. Likewise, certain consumer advocacy groups have singled out the pharmaceutical industry for charging exorbitant prices for many drugs. My take on the drug industry is that pharmaceutical manufacturers develop products to improve and, in many cases, save peoples' lives. The high price of the drugs is needed to recover the costs related to years of testing and developing these drugs. In addition, the companies must recover the costs associated with investigating the thousands of chemical compounds that did not make it out of the research clinic. In the course of my work I have met with many pharmaceutical executives and researchers and my impression is that most of them are motivated by their desire to advance science and develop life-improving and life-saving therapies. If they can earn a profit in the process, all the better.

In short, it is possible to find some fault with nearly every company. Many of these companies, however, also provide something worthwhile that renders them legitimate investment candidates. Where I draw the line is with companies whose practices are particularly egregious, such as polluters, or companies whose product does not have any redeeming value that might offset whatever harm is also associated with that product. Ideally, I would like to invest only in companies that are benefiting all of their constituencies—employees, customers, and the communities in which they operate. However, I believe that it is too restrictive and perhaps disingenuous to only invest in companies that are supposedly benefiting society. However, there are certain companies that I will not invest in, no matter how attractive their financial statements might be. I will not buy stocks in companies that pollute the environment or exploit their employees. I believe that in the long-term, companies that are managed without regard to ethics, will also prove to be poor performers. Malevolent companies may benefit in the short-term by saving on environmental measures or employee wages but over time, I believe these actions will result in the creation of such bad will with the public, that business will suffer. Simply, put, I believe that investors who invest in socially irresponsible companies are flirting with trouble.

In the end, decisions involving "what is good", are very personal and each investor should use his or her conscience and sense of right and wrong in determining which investments to pursue or avoid based on ethical considerations. I leave it up to you.

When To Sell

Almost as important as deciding which investments to get into, is deciding when to get out of the ones that you own. Generally, I am a proponent of buying and holding for the long-term. Good companies with good management tend to do well for long stretches of times. However, there are situations where investors should head for the exits.

Situations where the fundamentals have changed for the worse—Think about an investment 100 years ago where you might have owned 100 shares of the Acme Buggy Whip Company. Acme has excellent management, no debt, and great free cash flow. That's why you bought the stock after all. As long as people travel by horse and buggy, Acme will be a good investment. Can't go wrong. By the early 1900's, though, Acme probably would not be a very good investment. It might have been when you first bought it, but now cars, which were first viewed as a rich man's luxury, are being mass-produced for the average person. As an investor in Acme Buggy Whip, you can hold on to your investment or reconcile yourself to the fact that technological advances are making the horse and buggy, and your investment, obsolete. Clearly this is a situation where the fundamentals have changed for the worse. The key to holding on to your gains, or limiting your losses, is to be aware of changing fundamentals and to be honest with yourself and admit that the favorable attributes that caused you to buy the stock are fading or gone entirely. In such situations, it is usually best to sell. Some investors are reluctant to sell, particularly when they will be doing so at a loss. They feel it is not really a loss until the stock is sold. That is silly logic. An investment is a loss the moment that stock trades below your cost. That loss is there whether the stock remains in the portfolio or is sold. Never let your reluctance to realize a loss prevent you from selling an investment where the fundamentals have changed. One trick I use, is to ask myself whether I would purchase the same stock at the present time and current price if I did not already own it. If the answer is, "No", it is probably best to sell.

Excessive Valuation—In addition to situations where the investment fundamentals have changed for the worse, it is often wise to sell a stock, or any investment for that matter, when the price is so high that full or excessive valuation has been reached. Look back on our analysis of Costco Wholesale. At the end of our analysis we derived a price target based on certain metrics such as price to earnings and free cash flow. We set a target of $55 per share for Costco based on reasonable price to earnings and free cash flow multiples for the stock. If Costco shares were to rise suddenly above $55, it might be reasonable to conclude that the shares are fully valued and that future upside is limited. If the stock price were to rise further to $60, we might conclude that the shares are overvalued and we now have risk that the price will decline back to fair value. Should we sell our shares at this point? That depends. If the investment merits of Costco were unchanged and there was no fundamental reason to value the stock at a higher price-earnings or price to cash flow multiple, then the shares probably should be sold if they are trading well above our target price. Remember however, that target prices may increase over time as we use more recent numbers to calculate a fair value or target price for a particular stock. For example, we are assuming that Costco will earn $2.20 per share in 2005 and we are basing our target price, in part, on the stock being worth 25 times these earnings. If, after twelve months, Costco has in fact earned $2.20 per share in 2005, we may now estimate that Costco will earn perhaps $2.60 in 2006. If we expect the stock to eventually trade for the same 25 times this new earnings per share number, then we must adjust our target price upward to $65 per share (25x 2006 estimated earnings of $2.60 per share). It is important to keep in mind that targets need to be adjusted over time; upward if the company continues to meet or exceed earnings estimates, or downward if the company's results fall short.

When it comes time to sell, it is often hard to part with a stock that has done well, since investors may come to see it as invincible. Investors assume that what is going up will go up forever (remember the common mistake investors make when they base predictions on past results). Generally, I stay with my winners if I believe that the fundamentals will continue to be strong. If the reasons for originally buying the stock remain valid, I do not sell just because the stock may appear to be a bit expensive, as measured by price/earnings ratios, free cash flow yield, etc. However, there are times when the valuation clearly makes no sense. A good example of this occurred during the technology stock bubble of the late 1990's and 2000. Not all of these technology companies were fly by night start-ups. Some blue chip companies such as Intel, Microsoft, and Cisco Systems also reached bubble-level valuations. At one point Cisco Systems had a market capitalization of $500 billion dollars (larger than even ExxonMobil or General Electric) and the stock was valued at more than 80 times forward earnings estimates. It is not that investors should have sold Cisco because it was a bad company. Instead, they should have sold based on the fact that Cisco, despite being a good company, was selling at a valuation level that was completely unjustified. At the time, earnings were increasing at a rate of 30 percent a year. Certainly an impressive growth rate, but not high enough to justify a price of 80 times forward earnings estimates. In addition, investors should have kept in mind the law of large numbers that we discussed earlier. As companies grow very large, it becomes increasingly difficult to continue to grow at a rapid pace. With Cisco valued at $500 billion dollars, it was one of the largest companies in the world based on market capitalization. Investors should have realized that a $500 billion company cannot continue to grow at 30 percent for long.

I do not make these statements as someone with the benefit of hindsight. I firmly believed in the late 1990's that technology stocks were wildly overvalued and were due for a sharp drop. It was impossible to predict exactly when this would happen, but I was fairly certain, based on the principles discussed in this book, that it was better to sit on the sidelines than to take a crazy risk by buying these wildly overvalued stocks. Remember, don't be afraid to sell. Get out of your losers if the fundamentals have changed for the worse and do not be afraid to part with your winners if they have risen to a higher price than can be justified by the fundamentals such as earnings and cash flow valuations.

Investors should always be aware of the tax consequences of any stock sale that they may be considering. For example, if you are considering selling a stock that you have owned for ten months and have a large gain in the investment, it may be wiser to wait an additional two months so that the gain will be treated as a long-term capital gain and taxed at a lower rate.

Selling when the objective is to limit losses: stop-losses—a stop-loss is a technique that can be used to limit or stop further losses in a particular investment. The process is relatively simple. For example, an investor buys a $50 stock and wants to ensure that he or she will not lose more than 20 percent of the initial investment. Immediately after purchasing the shares, the investor tells his broker that he wants to put in a "stop-loss" order on the shares at $40. In the event that the stock drops to $40, the broker automatically sells the stock at $40. One advantage of a stop-loss order is that it forces the investor to be disciplined. Often investors buy stocks that go down and instead of realizing that they made a poor purchase decision and cut their losses, they hang on and hope and pray that the stock will rebound. More often than not, bad situations stay bad or even worsen. The best course of action is usually to admit that the initial purchase was a mistake, sell the stock, accept the loss, and look for better investment opportunities elsewhere. I am not suggesting that a 20 percent drop in a company's share price is proof that the company's underlying business is doing poorly and should be sold. However, often a stock's poor performance does reflect some underlying problem in the company's business.

A stop-loss order forces the investor to take the painful step of selling when the stock has met some predetermined loss limit. The second advantage of a stop-loss order is that the investor does not have to watch his or her stocks every day waiting and watching to see if the stock in question has hit the predetermined floor. A stop-loss order results in the stock being automatically sold when it hits the predetermined price. This is a useful feature for investors who do not watch their investments on a daily or even a weekly basis. Investors should be aware, however, that a stop-loss order will not protect the investor in the event that a company releases bad news that sends the stock price plummeting. When a stock "gaps down" from the previous day's closing price, the sale triggered by the stop-loss order will not occur at the pre-set price. Instead, the stock will be sold at the price where the stock opens for trading the next day. What is meant by "gap down" is as follows. Assume that our investor above, who bought shares of stock at $50 per share, and in the event that things do not go as planned, wants to limit his loss to 20 percent. He puts a stop-loss order at $40 with his broker. Over the next few months the stock drifts lower, settling at $41. After the close of trading the next day, the company announces that sales and profits will be much lower than investor expectations because its biggest selling product is being recalled due to a safety defect. Investors will be disappointed and many will want to sell their stock. Just because the stock closed at $41 the night before does not mean that it must open at that price the next day. Since there will be many more sellers than buyers, the stock will "gap down" to perhaps $38 or $37 or even lower, until there are buyers interested in purchasing shares given the bad news that has just been announced. Even though our investor has a stop-loss order that is supposed to be executed at $40, there are no willing buyers at $40 per share. The investor's stock will be sold at the opening of trading the next day, a price most likely in the 30's. It is important to realize that a stop-loss order is a good tool for maintaining discipline about exiting bad situations, but it cannot perform magic if a stock gaps down.

As an active, professional investor, I rarely have the need to use stop-loss orders, but I do recommend them for investors who are either indecisive or distracted from their investments, or both.

Exiting a cyclical business near the top—Several pages back we discussed the nature and characteristics of growth and cyclical stocks. For cyclical stocks, the key point to remember is that we want to buy these investments when times are bad but poised to recover. We want to sell them when times are still good but close to peaking. As should be obvious, these are not stocks that we want to own forever. As we discussed earlier, we want to buy these stocks when times are difficult but the end of the difficulty appears in sight. Remember that when we invest, we want there to be some coming catalyst that will get the stock price higher. A universal catalyst for cyclical stocks is the arrival of better economic times. If we feel that the economy is poised for recovery, we want to find cyclical companies to buy that will benefit from these better economic conditions. The reverse is true when economic times are very good. If we are holding cyclical stocks, we want to make sure that we get out of these companies before the economy has peaked and the next recession is at hand. This is no easy task since every time we read the newspaper, we are presented with economic data and the opinions of pundits who believe that the economy is about to take off or collapse. What we need to do is absorb this information and use our own common sense in deciding what we think is likely to occur in the next ten to twenty month period. It is important to accept the fact that when we aim to sell at the absolute high or buy at the absolute low, we will never be exactly right in timing these decisions. If we are, it was simply due to dumb luck. The key is to be close. If we purchased stock in a heavy equipment manufacturer such as Deere & Co. or Caterpillar, two classic cyclical companies, and the share price has doubled, and we are concerned that the economy may weaken in the year ahead, we should sell. It is okay if we are not precisely correct and the share price rises another twenty percent after we have sold. It is also ok if we hang on a little too long and sell after the stock has peaked and retreated ten or twenty percent from its high. We still have a large gain. The key is not to ride these stocks all the way back down.

Diversification Of Your Portfolio

I have a bit of a Jekyll and Hyde personality when it comes to diversifying my portfolio. In the mutual fund that I manage professionally, there is a fair amount of diversification. The fund holds investments in nearly every type of industry—healthcare, technology, energy, financial services, retail, etc.

In my personal portfolio, the level of diversification is far less. At the time of this writing, nearly two-thirds of my personal portfolio is invested in energy-related companies, since that is an industry that I believe will to do well in the foreseeable future. The remaining non-energy investments are very concentrated in several stocks in which I also have a high level of conviction. As a result of this lack of diversification, my personal portfolio is fairly volatile and does not track the performance of the broad stock market, as measured by the S&P 500 Index. There are many days when the S&P is up and my personal portfolio is down and vice versa. The upside, however, is that if I am correct in my analysis and predictions, my portfolio will do far better than the broader market. For example, this year the stock market, as measured by the S&P 500 Index, is up approximately four percent, whereas my personal portfolio is up in excess of twenty-seven percent.

The mutual fund portfolio that I manage professionally is fairly diversified because I am mindful of the fact that individuals who invest money in my Fund expect it to roughly track, and hopefully do better, than the major market indices such as the S&P 500. They are not looking to assume the risks associated with a very concentrated portfolio. As the portfolio manager, however, I do overweight certain areas such as energy-related stocks and buy significant positions in other companies that I believe will do well.

My advice to individual investors, is to take a middle of the road approach—do not be as concentrated as my personal portfolio, but do not be so diversified that your portfolio mimics the broad stock market. I recommend that investors own at least six different stocks in their personal portfolio. If you are first starting out and do not have much money to invest, it is ok to buy one or two individual stocks to start and also put some money into an exchange-traded fund that will add diversification to the portfolio. An exchange-traded fund is an investment such as the "Spiders" (*ticker symbol SPY*) that trades on a stock exchange and owns all the stocks in the S&P 500. In addition to the "Spiders", there are other broad-based exchange-treaded funds such as the NASDAQ 100 Index Tracking Stock which owns the 100 largest companies in the NASDAQ Composite Index. The ticker symbol for this fund is QQQQ. There are also exchange-traded funds, which hold shares in companies concentrated in a single industry. An example of one such industry-specific exchange-traded fund is the Pharmaceutical HLDRS Trust shares, which holds shares in companies in the pharmaceutical industry (ticker symbol PPH). Other industry specific fund shares include Biotech (ticker symbol BBH), Oil Services (OIH), Semiconductors (SMH), Retailers (RTH).… You can go to www.holders.com for a complete list of these industry-specific shares.

The advantages in owning these broad-based exchange-traded funds are several. If an investor has a relatively small amount of money to invest, the use of these types of shares enables him or her to have a diversified portfolio without having to buy more than two or three different stocks. Also, the industry-specific stocks allow investors to bet on a particular industry such as biotechnology, without worrying that they will pick the one or two companies that do poorly within that industry. When investing in risky industries such as biotechnology, it is more prudent to buy a basket of stocks instead of allocating all of your money to one company. Exchange-traded funds, such as the Biotech Holder shares are very useful for that purpose. The downside to these shares is that there is a management fee associated with them, and more importantly, they limit the investor's ability to make above average returns by doing the type of research and analysis that we have gone through in this book. I recommend that investors use these broad-based exchange traded funds in combination with individual stock investments.

In general, for investors with more than $20,000 to invest in stocks, I recommend that they own at least six stocks and no more than twenty. Obviously, by owning too few stocks, investors will have most of their eggs in just a few baskets. Is there a harm in owning many, many different stocks? Yes, there are several drawbacks to owning stocks of dozens of different companies. Individual investors who hold full-time jobs most likely do not have the time to adequately research and keep current on more than two dozen different holdings. In addition, my goal in investing, is to do better than the market averages such as the Dow Jones Industrial Average or the S&P 500. By owning many stocks, an investor increases the chances that his stock portfolio's performance will be no better or no worse than the market averages. Statistical studies have shown that as a sample size (the number of stocks in the investor's portfolio) approaches 30, it begins to behave very much like the population as a whole (the market averages). The upside to owning many stocks is that you should rarely do too much worse than the average. Perhaps I am an optimist or confident in my investment skills, because my goal is not to achieve average results, I want to beat the market averages.

Of course, when choosing stocks and diversifying your portfolio, it is important to not just own at least six stocks, but also to own stocks in a variety of different businesses. A portfolio of twenty stocks will not be considered properly diversified if all of the investments are in energy or healthcare companies. When diversifying among different industries it is not necessary to own a stock in every industry. Some industries such as the airlines and auto manufacturers are fundamentally bad businesses and should be avoided. I try to find the best companies in the best industries and aim to own one or two stocks in several different industries with the brightest outlook.

What To Avoid

Shorting stocks—Selling a stock short involves profiting from the decline in a company's share price. For those who are not familiar with the practice, shorting involves finding a stock that the investor believes is overvalued and borrowing those shares from an investor who owns them (brokers facilitate this process) and immediately selling those shares in the market and keeping the proceeds. The short seller is obligated to return those shares to the investor from whom they were borrowed, at some later date. The short seller hopes to return those borrowed shares by repurchasing them at a lower price at some point in the future. This may all seem complicated, but in practice, it is a simple process.

My advice to almost every investor is, "Do not waste your time shorting stocks." The risks are too great and, generally, the rewards are paltry. There are several reasons why this is usually the case. First, over time, stocks tend to rise. Some stocks do better than others, but as a group, stocks generally increase in price over multi-year periods. It was just over two decades ago that the Dow Jones Industrial Average broke above 1,000. Today, that average is above 10,000. Yes, there are periods when stocks, as a group, decline, but the periods when the stock market is falling are far fewer than those when the market is rising. By shorting a stock, you are paddling upstream, you are going against the general trend of the market, which is upward.

Investors who engage in short selling stocks argue that while they are going against the general trend of the market, they are only shorting individual stocks that they believe will fall. They contend that while the stock market as a whole may rise, they are betting that the stocks of the companies that they are short will decline. While this is true, there are several flaws in this argument. First, when the stock market is rising there is a general tide of optimism among investors that can lift all boats. Unless a company reports very poor results or there a specific negative event for that company, such as a product recall or corporate fraud, that company's share price is likely to rise along with the broader market. Second, assuming that the short seller makes the right call, and the stock does in fact go lower, the amount of the short seller's gain is limited by the laws of mathematics. Assume that a company's that manufactures videocassette recorders has a stock price of 30. A short seller bets against the company, correctly assuming that its business will be decimated by the arrival of digital DVD players. Even if the VCR manufacturer is so disastrously affected by the arrival of DVD players that it goes out of business and the share price goes to zero, the most that the short seller can make is 30 points, or double his investment. A stock price cannot go below zero. It cannot go down more than 100 percent. The short seller's maximum upside is 100 percent. That is certainly not a bad return, but you must remember that very few companies go bankrupt. The odds of finding the few that do are very low. More importantly, the risk associated with being wrong when shorting stocks is very high. Now go back to our example of the VCR manufacturer that is facing competition from DVD players. What if the VCR manufacturer sees this new threat and reacts to it by retooling its factories and begins to manufacture mp3 players? If the company can successfully transition its business into a new growth area and increase its earnings, the stock is likely to rise. If the company is able to sell millions of mp3 players and earn tens of millions of dollars, its share price may rise from 30 to 100 in the year or two following the transition. What happens to our short seller who bet that the share price would fall? He has lost 70 dollars on a 30 dollar "investment." He has lost over 200 percent of his money. As the stock rises, his initial 30 dollars disappears. He must come up with more cash or his brokers will forcibly "cover" his short sale by requiring him to buy back the shares he borrowed and sold short. If our investor wants to continue to be short the stock, he must come up with more money every time the VCR/mp3 stock rises. This may seem a bit confusing but the important point to remember is that the same laws of mathematics that limited the short seller's gain to 100 percent (the stock cannot go below zero) also dictate that the amount of a short seller's potential losses are infinite—the stock can double, triple, rise ten fold, etc). When you own a stock (also known as being "long" the stock) and bet that the share price will go higher, the most that you can lose is your initial investment. The stock price cannot fall below zero. The short seller, however, is faced with the prospect that the share price can rise ever higher, forcing him too come up with more and more money to cover the escalating losses. In summary, the short seller's upside is limited to 100 percent, but the downside is unlimited. That's a bad risk/reward tradeoff.

So to summarize, I do not recommend shorting stocks because generally stock prices move higher over time and it is not wise to fight this trend. Second, from an upside/downside, risk/reward tradeoff, the possible returns are heavily outweighed by the potential risks

Buying on margin—Buying on margin simply refers to the practice of purchasing stocks using borrowed funds. Under current rules, investors can put down as little as 50% of the purchase price when buying stocks. For example, if an investor wants to purchase 1,000 shares of a stock that is selling for $10 per share, he or she can put up $5,000 of their own funds and borrow the remaining $5,000 from the broker involved in the transaction. The broker likes to lend in these situations because they charge a fairly high rate of interest. In addition, the broker bears very little risk since the broker is holding the collateral for the loan (the shares of stock) and can immediately sell them if it wants to be repaid. The broker will also enforce what are known as margin requirements. The investor must always have at least 50% of the $10,000 loan in equity as collateral with the broker at all times. If the stock drops to $8 per share, there is only $3,000 of the investor's equity with the broker. ($8,000 of stock minus the $5,000 loan = $3,000 or 30% equity—a no, no) In this situation, the broker will call the investor and demand that he or she put an additional $2,000 in the brokerage account in order to maintain the 50% equity requirement. If the investor refuses, the shares will be immediately sold, the broker's loan will be repaid and the investor will be left with $3,000. Notice that the investor lost 40% of his investment despite the fact that the stock fell only 20%. The use of margin will magnify both gains and losses. It increases risk. Taking it one step further, if the stock falls to $2 per share, the investor will have lost $8,000 despite the fact that the size of the original investment was only $5,000. Not only can losses be magnified, but there also exists the risk that an investor can lose more money than he or she originally invested.

This use of debt to increase purchasing power and magnify gains and losses is known as leverage. In physics, leverage can be used to lift heavy objects such as large boulders that might otherwise be unmovable. Remember, however, that leverage works both ways. Sometimes the boulder remains stuck in the earth and the stick you are using for leverage breaks in your hand. It is prudent to avoid the use of margin.

Lessons from the Technology and Internet Stock Bubble of the Late 1990's

There are many lessons that should have been learned by investors following the market bubble in technology stocks that peaked in March of 2000 and popped in 2001. In addition to the billions of dollars that ordinary investors lost when the bubble burst, it was disappointing to see how many experienced investors who should have known better, were taken in by the market euphoria.

The bubble in technology stocks had its roots in two events, the advent of commercial activity on the Internet and the expectations for a huge wave in spending on computer hardware and software before the start of the year 2000.

By the mid-1990's, several companies pioneered the concept of selling commercial goods and services on the Internet. Companies such as AOL offered the ability to send instant mail to other Internet users. Amazon began selling books and CDs to consumers, allowing shoppers to browse for items from the comfort of their homes and enjoy the convenience of having purchases delivered to their residence.

As the Internet became an accepted medium to communicate instantly, get information, and shop, its use grew exponentially from one year to the next. New startup companies rushed in to try their hand at selling goods and services on the Internet. None of these companies were profitable at first, but many investors believed that eventually these companies such as Amazon, EBay, and Buy.com would not only change how consumers shopped but would also wipe out traditional retailers such as Barnes & Noble and the neighborhood grocery store. Who would spend precious time walking or driving to the bookstore when a selection could be found more conveniently on Amazon? Who would bother going to the grocery store when you could select your groceries online and companies such as Kozmo.com or Grocer.com would deliver the items to your home in a couple of hours or less? Investors drew a line between the "old" economy and the "new" economy. The old economy consisted of bricks and mortar retailers that would rapidly lose business to the new economy companies that offered speed and convenience. While nearly all of these "new" economy companies were losing money, optimistic investors took it for granted that at some point in the future, most would become profitable. How profitable? How large would the earnings be? That was anybody's guess. The sky was the limit. Investors sold old economy stocks despite their cheap valuations and loaded up on new economy stocks despite the absence of profits and any clear path to profitability.

Shortly after the emergence of the "new economy" euphoria, there came a phenomenon known as Y2K—Year 2000. It was believed by some that at the stroke of midnight on December 31, 1999, most of the world's computers would fail, as their internal calendars would be unable to comprehend the year 00. Forecasters claimed that planes would fall out of the sky, security systems would fail, bank ATMs would not function. Corporations, large and small, spent considerable amounts of money to ensure that their computer systems would continue functioning in the new millennium. This surge in the purchasing of new computer hardware and software resulted in sharp earnings increases for many technology companies and added to the speculative fever that was already present in the market for technology stocks.

The next spark for this rally in tech stocks was provided by the groups that I refer to as "The Facilitators", the Wall Street analysts, the media, and the corporate executives of these technology companies. Wall Street investment banks were earning huge fees by taking public scores of technology and Internet companies, most of which had limited operating histories and no record of profits. They had a vested interest in seeing that the bull market for these stocks continued. To that end, they saw to it that their research analysts who penned opinion reports on the very same companies that their investment bankers were taking public, wrote only in the most optimistic terms about these internet and technology companies. Whereas in the past, most of these research reports were objective and used traditional valuation methods to arrive at a target price for a company's stock, they now used outlandish methods or even none at all to derive wildly inflated target prices for the companies about which they wrote.

The media, especially television networks such as CNBC and programs such as Wall Street Week, loved the public fascination with tech stocks. Their audience increased tremendously. Publications such as *Business Week* and *Forbes* saw their subscriber ranks grow, as the stock market became a national pastime. The amount that they could charge for advertising rose. Like the Wall Street firms, they had a vested interest in seeing that this craze for technology stocks continued. Business programs on television would frequently have as guests, executives of Internet companies or the Wall Street analysts who wrote opinion reports about them. The executives would rarely miss a chance to talk of their companies in glowing terms and the boundless business opportunities that existed for them. What they were mum about, however, was when they would ever show a profit and rarely were they ever pressed too hard to give an estimate.

And the investing public bought into this. And why not; the pundits were saying buy, the analysts were saying buy, the stocks were going higher, neighbors were getting rich trading tech stocks, the new Internet frontier was at hand, and few were willing to risk being left behind. In early 2000, the tech stock-laden NASDAQ Index reached 5,000, more than seven times its low of 740, seen just five years earlier. How was it that just over a year later, that same Index would plunge below 2,000 and dip to 1,108 one year after that? Simply put, the stunning rise in technology stocks was a bubble. The stocks reached incredible valuations that were completely unsupported by the fundamentals. Buyers of these stocks were not investors, they were gamblers, buying something simply because it was going up. Eventually cracks began to appear in the façade of the Internet and technology companies. It became increasingly apparent that many of these Internet companies had no business plan; they had no credible path to ever achieve profitability.

As Internet companies ran out of cash, their stock prices began to fall. Once upward momentum began to falter, sellers piled on. After all, the main premise for buying these stocks, the simple fact that they were rising, was no longer valid. Buyers disappeared and sell orders flooded in. In any market where there are far more sellers than buyers, prices drop. Selling begot more selling. Companies ran out of cash and filed for bankruptcy. The selling continued and prices fell precipitously. After many months, stocks fell to a level where there was some value. Companies that were simply flights of fancy or frauds went of business. Investors in those companies lost everything. Other companies that were viable, but wildly overvalued merely saw their stock prices fall to levels that more accurately reflected their true value. Investor losses were tremendous. When the dust finally settled, some investors swore that they would never invest in the stock market again.

However, not all investors fared so badly. Those that were committed to investing based on fundamentals and common sense did not lose their shirts when the tech stock bubble burst. Let's review some of the issues we discussed earlier in this book and see where tech investors of the 1990's went wrong. I want you, the reader, to learn from the mistakes of the past. Perhaps it will be 20 or 30 years before another stock market bubble appears to rival the tech stock bubble of the late 1990's. Nonetheless, overvalued markets of one type or another are always present. Recently, real estate has threatened to replace technology stocks as the next can't-fail investment. The lessons from the tech stock crash are relevant to the current investment environment.

Most tech stock buyers in the late 90's did little fundamental research. Most probably never read through a 10-K or Proxy Statement or did any valuation analysis of the stocks that they purchased. Price target? Higher. Had these investors done any basic research, they would have seen that the companies they were buying were burning through cash, had no sound business plan or strategy, and were run by individuals with little prior experience. Granted, even had they conducted this research and been aware of these items, they might have shrugged off the warning and bought simply because the stocks, were rising. In addition, those speculators buying tech stocks gave absolutely no heed to valuation. Had they looked at where these stocks were trading as a multiple of earnings or free cash flow, they would have realized that any rationale for buying these stocks was indefensible. Ironically, the fact that most of these Internet companies had no earnings made it easier for speculators to ignore their outrageous valuations. Had they had even a slight amount of earnings, buyers would have had some measure by which to realize that these stocks were incredibly expensive. Instead, seeing only losses, buyers simply dismissed the whole concept of valuation. I hope that after reading this book, you will never be so bold, so greedy, or so foolish.

Where else did these speculators fail? Most ran afoul of The Bigger Fool Theory. They bought stocks merely on the expectations that a bigger fool would buy the same stock from them at a higher price. On March 10, of 2000, the market ran out of bigger fools. Speculators also expected results from the past to dictate the future. Another term for this might be momentum investing—the belief that something that is rising will continue to rise. The stock market does not necessarily follow the laws of physics. Bodies in motion do not always stay in motion. Never invest based on momentum and do not use past price movements to predict the future.

Another mistake that technology and Internet stock investors made in the late 1990's was their failure to diversify their portfolio. Many individuals with little or no investment experience jumped headfirst into technology stocks. Rather than build a diversified portfolio, these buyers simply bought what was working. They dismissed the possibility that the day would come when technology and internet stocks would no longer be the stars. A second group of buyers were investors who had some investing experience and held a diversity of stocks in their portfolios. Disappointed that their non-technology investments were lagging the performance of the tech stock laden NASDAQ, they sold their laggards and switched over to technology and Internet stocks. Many professional investors also fell victim to this. In the late 1990's, the performance of their diversified portfolios lagged the returns of the S&P 500 and the NASDAQ Composite Index. In an attempt to catch up, they over-weighted what was working (the technology stocks) and prayed for the best. They too felt the pain when the bubble burst. This group of investors should have known better and it is disappointing that individual investors who trusted these professionals to conservatively manage their savings, lost a great deal of their principal when the market collapsed. That is why I want you to understand the basics of investing. Even if you have others manage your savings, with a knowledge of investing, you will have the ability to monitor those you have trusted to manage your money.

Speculators in technology stocks in the late 1990's also made one of the classic investing mistakes, they were greedy when they should have been fearful. **If most of the participants in a market are greedy, it is probably wise to be fearful. If most of the participants are fearful, it is probably wise to be greedy.** Let me explain. If most investors are euphoric about technology stocks, it probably means that they have invested a large amount of their cash in that area. Stocks, or any investments for that matter, will rise in value as new buyers step in and push prices higher. If everyone is already in love with a particular stock or industry, there are probably few, if any, new investors who will come into the market, and create a further rise in price. A similar situation exists when most investors are fearful. If the majority of investors are pessimistic in their outlook for a particular stock or industry, they probably do not own stocks in that area. Stocks move lower when there are more sellers than buyers. If the vast majority of the crowd has already sold, there is less risk that new sellers will enter the scene and force the share price lower. This is not to say that just because a stock is hated by a majority of investors it should be bought. Very often things are hated because they are fundamentally bad investments. The stocks may be down but are probably going even lower. However, the best bargains are often found in the closeout bin, the stuff that no one wants. If the fundamentals are decent and the valuation very cheap, a bargain can become a big winner once the rest of the pack realizes that things are not as bad as they feared. In the late 1990's, technology investors blindly followed the crowd. Be an individual. Be an independent thinker.

Lastly, for all of the reasons mentioned above, it should be clear that perhaps the biggest mistake made by those who gambled with technology stocks in the late 1990's was that they abandoned the simple principles of **common sense**. Even if investors were novices and not familiar with the fundamentals of investing, they should have known that is not wise to invest large amounts of money in areas not well known to them. I realize that most readers will not remember every concept that is discussed in this book. However, I believe that if you take away the most important and simplest concept from this book, you will have gained something important. That concept is, **use your common sense**. Common sense may not find you the best investments, but more often than not, it will keep you out of trouble. Remember the Hippocratic Oath— first do no harm. Common sense is a valuable and under-appreciated asset.

Today's Bubble

Sadly, many of the same mistakes that were made by stock market speculators in the 1990's are being repeated today by real estate "investors". Real estate speculators today are buying properties whose rental income cannot even cover their costs of ownership. That should be a sign that the valuation is too high. Many property buyers have little knowledge about the fundamentals of real estate investing. There are buying because prices are moving higher. Since the fundamentals make little sense, speculators are buying with the hope that they can sell quickly to an even bigger fool. Speculators are following the herd.

They are greedy in a crowd that is greedy. They should be fearful. Where have we seen this before?

Lessons from the Collapse of Enron

As you may have gathered from the previous section, the late 1990's were a very exciting time in the stock market. Technology stocks were soaring. It seemed like everyone was getting rich speculating in one thing or another.

Enron, once a relatively conservative energy transport company, decided that they too wanted to capitalize on this era of speculation and financial boom. At the time, Enron owned and operated the largest gas pipeline system in the United States. The pipeline transported natural gas from the areas where it was produced, such as Louisiana, Texas, and the Rocky Mountains, to consumers in the rest of the United States. This was a very stable business but grew relatively slowly. Part of this pipeline business involved maximizing profits by transporting gas from regions in the country where supply was plentiful and prices low, to areas where supply was scarce and prices high. Enron wanted to expand this arbitrage-type business to other commodities besides natural gas. To that end, it bought an electric utility company in Oregon called Portland Gas & Electric.

Part of Enron's strategy was to sell Portland's electricity production in other areas in the United States that had higher electric prices. Once the company grew its gas and electricity trading operations, it expanded into other commodities that it believed it could trade profitably. The company borrowed billions of dollars to expand its trading operations. It also sold most of its "hard assets" such as the interstate gas pipeline, in an attempt to become a more profitable "virtual company", focused on trading. From the mid 1990's through 2000, Enron stock soared. The shares rose from just under eight dollars in 1992 to more than ninety in August of 2000. By late 2001, the company was bankrupt and the worthless shares were selling for a few cents a piece. What happened?

The simple answer is that once Enron abandoned its profitable gas pipeline business, for the alluring business of trading, which was not profitable, the company became a house of cards that collapsed when years of hidden trading losses eventually came to light. What ultimately put the company under, were rumors that much of the company's profits were fraudulent. As rumors of Enron's troubles spread, the stock price went from the 80's down to the 30's. Enron had borrowed billions of dollars to finance its operations. Some of the loans had provisions that stated that if the share price dropped below a certain dollar price, the company's lenders could immediately demand repayment of the loans. With the stock at $30, lenders demanded repayment. Enron could not produce the cash. This brought more scrutiny on the company and eventually it was discovered that the company had engaged in numerous transactions that created the illusion of profits when in fact the company was burning through cash year after year from the late 1990's until its demise in 2001. Investors in Enron's stock were wiped out; most of Enron's employees lost their jobs as well as much of their retirement savings which was invested in Enron stock.

The single most important lesson for investors from the Enron blowup is, "**Don't buy what you don't understand.**" I doubt that many, if any, investors who owned Enron stock truly understood the company's esoteric trading business and how those operations were earning their supposed profits. Enron's answers to questions ultimately came down to, "Trust us; we know what we're doing." Investors should never feel stupid if they don't understand a particular company's business or its operations. If, after reading company SEC filings, press releases, and conducting research on the Internet, you still cannot understand the company and how it makes money, move on. There are thousands of other companies from which to choose. Do not feel compelled to invest in a company you do not understand simply because the share price is moving higher. Invest in good fundamentals, not momentum.

Investors, when evaluating Enron should have been a little turned off by the company's management. Company executives were regarded as arrogant, particularly in response to any questioning of the company's operating practices. That arrogance was often seen as deserved, given the meteoric rise in the company's stock price. Apart from the arrogance, investors should have been concerned by the company's promotional attitude regarding the supposed value of the company's stock. Top executives would routinely appear in interviews to talk about how high they expected the stock to eventually go. Just before the onset of bankruptcy, CEO Ken Lay can be seen on a videotape dismissing concerns about the company's financial health and claiming that the share price was undervalued. At the time, the stock carried a double-digit price tag. Within a few months it would be close to zero. I believe it is best to **avoid management that is overly promotional.** A solid and capable management team will let their actions and results speak for themselves. Those results should cause the stock price to rise. Enron investors should have been a little leery of a management team that saw fit to aggressively promote themselves and the company's stock.

The collapse of Enron helped bring to light the issue of biased research reports that are published by many Wall Street brokerage firms. Throughout Enron's decline, analysts from most of the major brokerage firms urged investors to buy shares of Enron stock. Many investors heeded this advice and purchased more and more Enron stock as it fell, on the foolish advice that successively lower share prices represented an increasingly better buying opportunity. What many of these investors failed to grasp was the fact that many of these analysts had conflicted interests when making investment recommendations on companies such as Enron. In its pursuit of growth and expansion, Enron borrowed billions of dollars and sold tens of millions of new shares of stock. Most of these bond and stock offerings were underwritten (sold to the public) by brokerage firms such as Merrill Lynch. These firms made tens of millions of dollars in fees from these underwritings. The firms were always eager for more business from Enron. If their research analysts were to write negative research reports about the company, Enron would most likely drop that brokerage firm when it came time for a new offering of stock or bonds. Enron was smart enough to spread its investment banking (underwriting) business among many firms so that each firm's analysts would write positive research reports on the company.

The chorus of analyst's voices urging investors to buy Enron was no accident or coincidence. In addition, many of the brokerage firm's analysts received a large portion of their pay from the investment banking fees that their firms received from companies such as Enron, the same companies about whom they were writing so-called unbiased research. Write a favorable report, receive investment banking fees, and get a big year-end bonus. It is no wonder why so few analysts were negative on Enron even as the company's serious problems became more apparent. It was not until nearly the very end, when Enron's stock reached the low-single digits, down over 90 percent from its high, that most analysts lowered their ratings from "buy" to "sell"—not very helpful. Unfortunately, most investors were unaware of these inherent conflicts that rendered worthless most of these analyst reports. Certainly, some analysts produce useful research but **it is important that investors be able to do their own research.** That is the purpose of this book. It allows you to make well-informed decisions and not rely on the advice of others whose own interests may conflict with yours.

Had investors done their own research on Enron, they would have seen that despite the company's impressive reported earnings growth in the late 1990's, **Enron never reported one cent of free cash flow.** The company was in constant need of additional cash to fund expansion or for use as collateral in its trading operations. This should have been a red flag, warning investors that something was not right. Enron's supposed earnings were a fiction. The company was recording money received from loans as income and using other tricks to make income appear where there was none. It is important that investors focus on earnings **and** free cash flow **and** the balance sheet. It is important that investors seek out companies that are increasing earnings and also generating free cash flow and are not burdened by large amounts of debt. Had investors followed this discipline they most likely would have steered clear of Enron.

Use Your Common Sense And Avoid Hard-Sell Pitches

Coming up with good investment ideas is not the same as developing the theory of relativity. I am of the belief that most people who possess average intelligence and a good deal of common sense can do well in the stock market. I cannot stress enough the importance of using common sense. If a potential investment that a broker or some tout proposes sounds too good to be true, it probably is. If you have a reasonable amount of intelligence, an investment idea should make sense to you. You should be able to understand the potential upside and the possible risks. All investments have risks. If you cannot see any, you are missing some angle. Keep digging for information and keep asking questions until you can quantify what the risks are. Don't ever let someone try to convince you that an investment is without risks. No such situation exists.

There are very few instances in life where we must make quick decisions on matters of importance. There are times, perhaps during a medical emergency, when we must make quick decisions and rely on someone else's information and advice, without fully understanding all the issues surrounding our decision. That should never occur with investing. An investment that is good today will still be good tomorrow or even a week from now. If someone is putting pressure on you to invest now or lose a great opportunity, it is almost always a bad deal. If people don't want you to do a reasonable amount of research and investigation, chances are they are hiding something from you. Be very suspicious of hard-sell pitches. In fact, a good rule of thumb would be to avoid them entirely. Unlike the medical decision that must sometimes be made in haste, there is rarely a good reason to invest in a hurry. There is always a safe place to put money until you check up on a research idea. There is nothing wrong in keeping money in savings accounts, money market funds or Treasury bonds until you find the right investment.

Red Flags And Other Pitfalls To Avoid

Insider selling—Be careful when you see that insiders (company executives and directors) have recently sold large amounts of their own company's stock. There are often legitimate reasons why an insider might sell stock—diversification, purchase of a home, approaching retirement, etc. However, beware when a top executive owns $100 million of his own company's stock and sells $60 million of it within a short period of time. There are no home purchases that would justify such a large stock sale. Presumably, company insiders have the best sense of the future performance of their own company. Their decision to significantly reduce their holdings should be seen as a warning sign. Conversely, large purchases by insiders can provide some evidence that the outlook for the company and its stock is favorable. All insider purchases and sales must be disclosed on a statement called a Form 4 that is filed with the SEC (Securities and Exchange Commission). These filings are public and available to individual investors.

Small or nonexistent ownership by insiders—This red flag is related to the above issue of insider selling. If an executive does not have the conviction to invest a large percentage of his wealth in the company that he manages, why should you? It is not a good sign when an executive earns the vast majority of his compensation in cash and is not required to own stock in his own company. Remember from our Costco example that one of the attributes that I liked about Costco management was that most of their compensation came in the form of stock and options that they were holding for the long-term. By holding this stake in their company, they were implicitly expressing their belief that the share price would move higher over time. Remember, we want management to put their money where their mouth if. If their company is such a good investment, we want to see insiders buying and owning shares.

Relatives or friends of the CEO in management or on the Board of Directors—Remember from our Costco and Overstock.com examples, the importance of reading about the members of management and the Board in the 10-K and the Proxy Statement. We want to know who these people are. My concern in seeing relatives or friends of the CEO on the same management team is that it smacks of nepotism. If the CEO is doing a poor job and his or her father is the chairman of the Board of Directors, is it realistic to believe that the Board will remove the CEO? Often, friends of the CEO sit on the Board of Directors of the company and determine important matters such as whether he or she is doing a good job, compensation, and whether the CEO will continue as the chief executive. There are many instances of poor-performing CEO's who are lavished with generous pay packages and kept on despite many years of poor performance. It can be tricky to read through the 10-K and Proxy Statement and determine if a Board member is a friend of the CEO. I try to see if there are any Board members who look like they don't belong. For example, several years ago, investors complained that Michael Eisner, the CEO of The Walt Disney Company, stacked the Board of Directors with friends who treated him a little too kindly. One of the Board members was the principal of the school that his children attended. In reading the 10-K, investors should have questioned why a Southern California school principal was on the Board of a large public company. As our example above with Overstock.com showed, it is not too difficult to read a 10-K and Proxy Statement and get a sense of whether the Board is truly independent and looking out for shareholders, or if the Board is in the pocket of management. A nose for sleuthing and a little common sense will serve you well.

Succession by a relative—This red flag is slightly different from the previous danger sign. Even if the CEO has no friends or relatives on the Board of Directors, we do not want to see a lower ranking executive and heir apparent, who is related to the current CEO. Many companies, despite being public, are often controlled by the family that founded, or owns a large stake in the company. The general public also owns stock in the company, but the CEO or his family control the company through their large ownership of shares or through their ownership of a special class of shares that have greater voting power then the shares available to the general public. Examples of such companies are Ford Motor, The New York Times, Coors Brewing, Qualcomm, and many, many others. Even though Ford Motor was founded by Henry Ford nearly a century ago and despite the fact that Ford family members own far less than a majority of the outstanding shares, as a single voting bloc they can effectively control the Board and management of the company. It is no wonder then that the current CEO of the company has the last name of Ford. It is no wonder that the New York Times Company is controlled and run by the Sulzberger family, whose ancestor purchased the newspaper more than 100 years ago. It is also no wonder that these stocks have performed very poorly year after year and yet there is little pressure to change the company's top management. Many large companies have nepotism rules that prohibit the hiring of relatives. Beware of companies that act as employment factories for favored relatives. Investors should ask the question, "When Ford Motor chose a new CEO, was William Ford the best possible candidate available or was he chosen because of his family's influence?" If you think he was the absolute best candidate available, then you must appreciate the fact that it is quite an incredible coincidence that he also happens to be a Ford. My advice—stay away from family controlled companies; stay away from companies where the hand-picked successor is a relative of the current CEO. Although no corporation is a true democracy, try to find the ones that most resemble a democracy, where top positions are acquired by merit rather than appointment.

Never buy stocks of companies in bankruptcy—Almost by definition, the value of a share of stock of a company that has declared bankruptcy is zero.

Completely worthless. Inexperienced investors are often lured into buying shares of bankrupt companies since these shares usually trade for anywhere from a few cents to just over one dollar per share. Sometimes the gambling desire takes over and investors believe that if they buy a stock for a dollar and if it rises by a mere fifty cents, they have made a whopping fifty percent on their "investment." Also, investors see a bankrupt company, such as an airline, continuing to operate with airplanes and other assets, and assume that since the company controls and operates these assets, there must be some amount of value in the share price. This false assumption is often what trips up many investors. Companies can continue to operate despite being bankrupt. Even though they continue to operate their assets, those assets are no longer owned by the shareholders. The assets, and just about anything else of value, belong to the bondholders and other parties, such as banks, to whom the bankrupt company owes money. Here's why—companies usually go bankrupt because they have taken on too much debt and can no longer make the interest payments on that debt or cannot repay that debt when it comes due. When that happens, banks or bondholders who are owed money by the corporation, seek to have the company declared bankrupt. In bankruptcy, these same banks and bondholders take control of the company. They now own all the assets of the company. There is almost never anything left for the stockholders.

There are only a handful of instances where a company declared bankruptcy and shareholders received anything other than a tax deduction. What often confuses investors is that when they see a company forced into bankruptcy, the stock plunges to pennies and then several months or a year later, the company emerges from bankruptcy and the stock is trading again at a price of perhaps ten or twenty dollars. Many investors assume that they missed a great opportunity to make a fortune by buying the shares for pennies when the company went bankrupt and then selling them at a much higher price after the company emerges from bankruptcy. Here is the mistake they are making—when a company goes through bankruptcy, its shares are cancelled. They no longer exist once the company emerges from bankruptcy. Bondholders and other creditors, such as banks and suppliers, own the entire company. To recoup a portion of the money owed to them, they exchange their IOU's for "new" shares in the company. The bondholders cancel the debt that is owed to them in exchange for this "new" stock. Much of this stock is then sold to new investors in an IPO (initial public offering). The money taken in from the IPO is used compensate the bondholders for the debts that were owed to them. The company then emerges from bankruptcy. Free of debt and no longer bankrupt, the company can try to operate profitably, and perhaps, with new management may succeed. The "new" stock in the company bears no relation to the old bankrupt shares that were trading for just a few pennies. Kmart is a good example of this process. The retailer went bankrupt and debt holders took control of the company. They closed poor performing stores and cancelled the debt that was owed to them. They also took other steps to cut costs and improve operations. The company emerged from bankruptcy, new stock was issued, which then rose sharply until it eventually hit $100 per share. Several months ago, a friend lamented to me that he wished he had bought Kmart stock when they first declared bankruptcy and the shares were selling for fifty cents. I explained to him that had he done that, his stock would have been cancelled when the company emerged from bankruptcy and he would have lost all of his money. He would not have been a shareholder in the "new" Kmart that emerged from bankruptcy and hit $100. That was "new" Kmart stock. The stock that traded for pennies was "old" Kmart stock which was subsequently cancelled as worthless. What he needed to do was buy Kmart stock right AFTER it emerged from bankruptcy. Then he could have participated in the stock's ride up under new management. Please, please, please, avoid the temptation to buy stock in companies that have declared bankruptcy. In most instances, you will be left with nothing.

Be wary of stocks selling for under $5—Most companies come public at a price in the $20–$30 range. For a stock to get below $5, most likely something very bad happened to the company to cause the share price drop by 50, 60, or 80 percent. True, circumstances may change for the better and the company may recover, but investors need to really do their homework, and even then, only invest a small portion of their portfolio in these risky situations. Many inexperienced investors assume that stocks trading at three, four, or five dollars are somehow "cheap." Several months ago, I recommended the stock of the organic grocer, Whole Foods Markets, to my brother-in-law. At the time, the stock was selling for $100 per share. My brother-in-law is an intelligent guy but he could not understand how I could recommend a stock that was selling for $100. He kept repeating that it was too expensive and how could he expect to make money in a stock that was already at 100. I tried to get him to ignore the dollar price of the stock. After all, as you, the reader, now know, a stock is only truly expensive if it is selling at a very high multiple of earnings or free cash flow. A stock selling for $100 but earning $5 per shares is far cheaper than a $6 stock with earnings of 10 cents per share. That $6 stock is not cheap at all. It's very expensive. Some investors are attracted to three, four, and five-dollar stocks because they like the notion of being able to own many shares and naively believe that if the share price increases by "just" one or two dollars, they will make a quick thirty, forty or fifty percent. The errors in this logic should be obvious. First, the absolute number of shares owned is irrelevant. What matters is the size of the investment, in dollars. In addition, a low-priced stock that increases one or two dollars, resulting in a large gain, can just as easily fall one or two dollars, resulting in a quick and steep loss. Please keep this in mind when the siren song of the low-priced stock tries to lure you. Remember, low price usually means risky, not cheap.

Fads and manias—Investing in stocks that are on a tear because of a recent fad or mania flies in the face of many of the lessons that we should have learned after the technology bubble burst in 2000. Anyone who invested in a hula hoop company in the 1970's will tell you, "avoid fads." It is important that investors not confuse an emerging trend with a fad. An emerging trend is the dawn of some change that will become more pervasive and is expected to have staying power. A fad is something that comes from out of the blue, takes off like a rocket, and disappears as quickly as it arrived. An emerging trend today would be the increasingly popularity of organic food products. Organic food has been around for over two decades and its popularity has been on the rise, but it is only recently that it has achieved more mainstream acceptance. This emerging trend is an investable theme. Companies such as Whole Foods Markets, Wild Oats, and United Natural Foods will all benefit from this trend. Extremely low-rise jeans for women, however, are a fad. They look stupid, and two years from now no one will admit to ever having owned a pair.

Absurd valuation—Every investment, no matter how good its fundamentals, must also make sense from a valuation perspective. When stocks sell at price to earnings ratios above 100, there is almost no way that earnings can ever increase enough in the coming years for the stock price to move much higher. At that level of valuation, the stock already reflects all the positive news that might come in the future. Owning stocks with such high valuations involves a great deal of risk. If news and earnings reports are ever anything less than spectacular, the stock will fall precipitously. There is no set cutoff for the maximum price to earnings ratio or price to free cash flow ratio that an investor should pay. If the fundamentals are excellent and the company is growing rapidly, it is not necessarily foolish to pay 50 times earnings or to purchase stock in a company that has no free cash flow. One of my favorite stocks this year has been Whole Foods Markets, which sells for just over 50 times the preceding year's earnings. While I admit that this high valuation scares me a little, I believe that the fundamentals are strong enough to support this lofty price/earnings ratio. If a company is at the very early stages of its growth, it may be acceptable to pay a very high price for the relatively small earnings. However, if the company is fairly large, it is doubtful that the company will be able to grow that much more from its already sizeable base to justify such a high price. Generally, I avoid stocks selling at extremely high p/e ratios.

Avoid Stocks of Companies Led by CEO's that are Overpaid, Promotional or Have Checkered Pasts—A discussion of chief executive pay could take up as many pages as this entire book. It is my opinion that the vast majority of top executives of public companies in the United States are shockingly overpaid. Top executives often take home pay that is hundreds of times the salary paid to the average employee at the companies they head. These obscene pay packages have the effect of destroying employee morale and increasing the economic divide between the haves and have-nots in the United States. Almost without exception, these huge pay packages are unwarranted. First, there is little relationship between pay and performance. Executives at large corporations are paid vast sums despite mediocre performance, as measured by the increase in company earnings or the increase in the company's stock price.

Second, most CEOs are not performing any task that could not be done by another individual at a much lower price. In other words, they are not being paid a free market salary. They are being paid what their friends and cronies on the Board of Directors are willing to lavish on them. Many Americans complain about the multi-million salaries paid to professional athletes. However, these salaries were earned in a true free market. The team's owner is trying to spend as little money as possible since it is his money being used to pay the salaries. In addition, a team owner will generally not pay a player more than he thinks the player will earn for the team in the form of increased ticket sales and increased television revenue. Lastly, the athlete is performing a task that few others can do. He cannot be easily replaced. Few among us can hit 90 mile per hour fastballs, let alone a curveball. A chief executive, on the other hand, is paid huge amounts for reasons that are far less clear. Unlike the athlete, the executive is not paid directly by the owner. The chief executive's pay is determined by the Board of Directors, which is not using its own money to pay the CEO. Also, the CEO may be the friend of other Board members or often sits on the Board of a company where another Board member is the CEO and therefore is in a position to return the favor to them.

Unlike the athlete, who is paid for performing at a certain level, for example, hitting a certain number of home runs, throwing touchdowns, etc., the CEO's pay is often arbitrary and uniformly high, and bears no relation to performance. Unlike the athlete who can do something that few others can, the ability to run a corporation is probably not nearly as unique a skill as throwing a football to a moving target forty yards away, while wearing heavy pads and a helmet, all the while being chased by 275 pound men who want to pound you. Many large, established companies virtually run themselves. They are not led by brilliant or creative leaders. The person at the helm is relatively interchangeable and there is no need to pay that person an amount of compensation three hundred times what the average employee at the same company is earning.

Lastly, an athlete who performs poorly is benched or sent to the minor leagues, or cut from the team. Executives who produce poor results tend to stay in their positions for many years until they retire or are finally forced out by the Board of Directors. Even when CEO's are forced to leave, they depart with multi-million dollar severance packages, generous pensions and other benefits that keep them in comfort for the remainder of their lives.

Unfortunately, investors in most companies are forced to accept the fact that excessive CEO pay is simply par for the course. What I generally try to avoid are companies led by CEO's whose pay packages are so large as to be outrageous even when measured against the pay of other chief executives. Huge pay packages are a red warning flag for several reasons. First, any Board that awards an undeserved and outsized compensation scheme to top management is not truly independent. Either the Board is incompetent or is rewarding a crony. You should be aware that many CEO's sit on the Boards of other public companies. CEO's of those companies sit on other corporate Boards. Many of these relationships are like an interwoven spider's web. Board members will often pay a CEO an outsized sum so that the favor will be returned to them when their Board decides what their pay should be. In addition, many CEO's reward Board members with generous stipends, company stock and options, and other benefits that prevent the Board members from making objective decisions when setting the CEO's pay. It is important to invest in companies with a truly independent Board. Excessive CEO pay is a sign that this criterion is not being met. The purpose of the Board is to oversee the top executives for the benefit of the shareholders. It is not in the best interests of shareholders when the Board is too cozy with top management. Finally, it may simply be bad policy to invest in a company led by an individual motivated by unbridled greed. Greed may stand in the way of sensible business decisions and may lead to a strategy of excessive risk-taking that can threaten the financial health of the company.

Greed is not the only vice to be wary of when examining a company's management. Generally, I am suspicious of managements that are overly promotional. In my experience, I have found that most successful management teams are *quietly* effective. They under-promise and over-deliver. A CEO's promises that turn out to be hollow, destroy management credibility and cause investors to flee the stock, sending the share price lower. Good management teams let their accomplishments speak for them. Most of the companies whose stocks I have owned for a long time, such as Whole Foods Market, Teva Pharmaceuticals, Medtronic, Costco, and others, are led by management teams that set conservative goals and usually exceed those targets when they report results. I can think of many companies such as Tyco, Cendant, and Enron whose stocks have done terribly, that I was fortunate enough to avoid, in part because the promotional nature of the top executives turned me off.

Lastly, avoid shares of companies whose CEO's have had brushes with the law or other past ethical lapses. A simple Internet search can provide a wealth of information about an executive's past accomplishments or misdeeds. I am not suggesting that individuals who have erred in the past are destined to return to a life of crime. However, with thousands of companies listed on the New York Stock Exchange, NASDAQ, and the American Stock Exchange, there are enough choices that we can easily invest in companies led by executives with unblemished records. Of course, an honest dummy is not the ideal CEO, but it is not hard to find companies led by upstanding and talented individuals.

Faith versus Conviction—Have Conviction, Avoid Faith; Do not Have an Ego—While it is sometimes a virtue to have faith—faith in your spouse, family, the home team…., **it is destructive to have faith in your investments.** It is important, to **have conviction,** conviction gained through thorough research and an understanding of what you are purchasing. To buy something on faith is no different from gambling. It reduces the investment decision to a coin toss. Even if the investment decision is well-researched and done with conviction, you must always be aware of changing conditions that may render the original investment decision invalid. It is important that you not continue to hold onto an investment merely because you have faith that it will turn profitable. It is important that investors abandon faith and rely solely on the fundamentals associated with a particular investment and their own good judgment. To lose faith in an investment is not a sin. Investors should be honest with themselves, and sell investments that are mistakes and have no reasonable chance of rebounding. As I mentioned earlier, I often ask myself if I would purchase the same the same stock at the present time at the current price if I did not already own it. If the answer is, "No", it is probably best to sell.

In addition to faith, another impediment to good investment decisions is an oversized ego. It is important that investors be honest with themselves at all times. If a decision to buy a particular stock turns out to have been made in error, it is important that you be honest with yourself and admit that a mistake was made. It is usually best to sell a stock when it first becomes apparent that the fundamentals are not as good as originally thought. We all make bad investment decisions. I have made many. One of the things that has made me a better investor over the years, is that I have learned to quickly get out of investments with deteriorating fundamentals. Some investors have egos that make it impossible for them to admit that they made a mistake. Instead they continue to hold on and watch a small loss become a large one. **Do not allow your ego to control your investment decisions.** If the investment was made in error, or the fundamentals have changed materially, admit it and look for better opportunities elsewhere. Do not hold on because of pride, ego, or faith. Nip problems in the bud and find better alternatives elsewhere. There are thousands of stocks from which to choose. Do not hang on to too many losers.

Don't be seduced by yesterday's winners—It is said that most military preparations for future conflict are based on the previous war that was fought. After World War I, the French built the Maginot Line, a fortification perimeter around most of the country. This defense was expected to repel any foreign invasion. Shortly after the start of the Second World War, however, the Maginot Line proved to be a complete failure in its ability to stop the German army. The French designed the fortifications to defend against World War I armament such as slow, heavy tanks and foot soldiers. The defense was completely inadequate against airplanes and fast-moving vehicles. The Maginot Line was useless and a colossal waste of money. The French prepared themselves to re-fight the prior war and were completely blind to what the future might bring.

The same is true when investing. Too often, investors look to what worked in the past when trying to figure out what will work in the future. After technology stocks collapsed following their tremendous run-up from 1995 through 2000, investors continued to pour money into the stocks of these same companies, believing that they would quickly rebound. When the stocks failed to recover, investors threw even more money at them, assuming that it was only a matter of time before this same group would once again lead the market higher. While these speculators were trying in vain to resurrect the dead, a whole new segment of the market was taking off—shares of long-forgotten value stocks in industries such as energy, retailing, hospitals, and insurance companies were hitting all-time highs.

The fact is, every market cycle is different. In the late 1980's through early 90's large growth companies such as pharmaceutical manufacturers, supermarket companies, and consumer products manufacturers such as Proctor & Gamble and Kellogg were the market leaders. In the late 1990's stocks of technology and communication companies led the way. After the bubble in those stocks popped, value stocks took the lead. At the time of this writing, energy companies such as ExxonMobil and Schlumberger are the market darlings.

The group that led the past up-cycle is no more likely to be the leader in the years to come than any other group of stocks. Therefore, it is unwise to chase yesterday's winners. It is important to remain focused on current conditions and the outlook for the future. It is important to use all of the tools discussed above—an emerging theme or trend, positive and improving fundamentals, and attractive valuation. Those factors and not some repetition of the past, will lead you to tomorrow's winners.

Afterword

What To Do With Your Profits And Other Bits Of Advice

Now that you have endured my preaching about investments, please bear with me for one final friendly lecture. The following maxims have little to do with investing or finance but are simply some thoughts that I wanted to share with the reader. I hope that after reading this book you will find increased success with your investments. If this brings you greater prosperity, I hope that you will be generous with others. Most Americans are generous, but it should not take acts of terrorism or a series of hurricanes to motivate us share with others in need. In addition to donating money, it is important that people donate other items, such as time, or more physical and personal items such a pint of blood, bone marrow, or even organs upon our death to help those who may be in desperate medical need. Being comfortable is not a sin, but is important to remember that many events that enrich and impoverish us happen by chance. We should not look down on people who have less than us, or believe that success, if achieved, is the fulfillment of an entitlement.

One way to have more money to spend on others is to lavish less on oneself. I am hardly suggesting that you take a vow of poverty, but it is troublesome to see ostentatious displays of wealth in nearly every corner of the country. People live in 6,000 square foot homes when a dwelling half that size will suffice. Large SUV's seem to have replaced cars simply because drivers want to sit high up and regal in their massive vehicles. Not only do these three-ton behemoths waste fuel and pollute the air, but they are a danger to the occupants of more reasonably-sized cars in the event of a collision. Modesty is a virtue both in terms of how we choose to live and how we project ourselves.

In addition to living more modestly, we need to be less consumed with seeking status, and abandon the culture that celebrates fame and wealth while ignoring the real heroes in our lives. I am amazed that people fawn over celebrity hucksters such as Donald Trump, and Martha Stewart, who contribute little to the betterment of mankind. I am amazed that people bother to know the most minute details of celebrities' lives but are unconcerned or unaware of circumstances that affect loved ones or neighbors. It is important that we not confuse fame with virtue. We should be aware of prominent people but save the adoration for real heroes, those who have accomplished truly great things, and others in our lives, who love and support us. Celebrities should rarely be viewed as heroes. The real heroes in our lives are the firemen in our towns and cities, the researchers working, away from the limelight, to cure serious diseases such as cancer, diabetes, and multiple sclerosis. Soldiers who join the military at great risk to themselves and little pay, deserve our respect and support. So do the teachers who go the extra mile to pull up a lagging student or motivate a class. There are many volunteers who give of themselves to make our communities better. All these people are the real heroes in our lives. One of my heroes has always been my dad, who saved my life during a sledding accident when I was a young boy. He taught me to be honest and hard-working and to treat people fairly. My mom is also my hero who instilled in me a concern for the environment and a love of animals.

She taught me that most animals are inherently kind creatures who often need our protection. Be kind to the pets in your home and if you don't have any, consider adopting a needy pet from your local shelter. If you cannot have a pet, support your local Humane Society or other animal shelter by donating money or your time. As far the animals in the wild, it is important that we maintain reserves where they can live in order to maintain the diversity of life on the planet. Animals such as grizzly and polar bears, bison, and many others, face threats to their natural habitats. It is important that we maintain open lands when they can live. To that end, it is essential that we protect the environment. As the world's population continues to swell, putting additional pressure on the supply of clean air and water, it is imperative that we improve the condition of the planet. Whether or not global warming is being caused by pollution is a subject of controversy. However, there can be no debate that the quality of the earth's air and water is in decline. Many fish contain high levels of mercury and pollutants contaminate groundwater. A recent visit to Sequoia National Park in California confirmed to me that we need to do more to protect the environment. Even on a cloudless day, the views of the surrounding mountains were obscured by the haze of small pollutant particles in the air.

In addition to being concerned about others and our environment, take care of yourself. If you smoke, stop. Throw out your cigarettes and never buy another pack again. If you need motivation to quit, visit the oncology ward in any large hospital and see first-hand how unpleasant and frightening cancer is.

Exercise. If gyms bore you, ride a bike, rollerblade, ice skate, play tennis, cross country ski or swim. Cut down on red meat consumption and foods high in fat. A longer and better quality of life will be your reward. Plus you'll look and feel great. What better to go with your investment wealth than the longevity and health to enjoy it. Also, use some of your investment gains to travel. See America the beautiful or learn about other cultures in other countries.

Lastly, we are our brothers' keepers. Treat your family, friends, neighbors and strangers with kindness and generosity. It has become very apparent in the new millennium that Americans need to look after one another.

Terms And Definitions

Balance Sheet—A corporation's balance sheet is a snapshot of the company's assets, liabilities, and shareholder's equity taken on a set date. The balance sheet gets its name from the fact that assets must equal liabilities plus shareholder's equity. When these items equal, they are in balance. Assets include such items as cash, inventory, buildings, and money owed to the company. Liabilities include debt that the company owes to banks or bondholders. The excess of assets over liabilities is shareholder's equity. If liabilities exceed assets, the company may be bankrupt, and shareholder's equity has a zero or negative value.

Bullish/Bearish—A bull is someone who expects a particular stock or the stock market as a whole, to move higher. A bear is one who is pessimistic about a particular stock or the market as a whole, and expects them to move lower. According to lore, the terms came about from the way each animal attacks its enemies. A bull attacks and pushes its horns higher, whereas a bear swats it huge paws downward.

Depreciation—Depreciation is a non-cash expense that is incurred over the useful life of an asset that is expected to last for more than one year. For example, if a company purchases a truck in 2005 for $20,000, and the truck is expected to have a useful life of five years, the company will incur a $4,000 depreciation charge each year for the five-year life of the truck. It is important to remember that depreciation is a non—cash charge. The cash charge of $20,000 was incurred in 2005 when the truck was purchased. The $4,000 per year depreciation expense attempts to spread the recognition of the cost of the truck over its five-year useful life.

Economic Cycle—This term refers to the expansion and recession of the economy. During times of recession, companies generally lay off employees, consumer spending declines, and confidence in the economy is low. During recessions, interest rates tend to fall, which eventually leads to increased borrowing as the cost of borrowing (interest expense) is reduced. Increased borrowing leads to increased spending, as the proceeds from the loans are put to productive use. This increased spending leads to the creation of new jobs, an increased confidence in the economy, which leads to increased consumer spending and additional job creation and economic expansion. This cycle from recession to expansion and back to recession is the economic cycle.

Exchange Traded Funds—Also known as ETFs, Exchange Traded Funds, are a type of fund whose investment objective is to achieve nearly the same return as a particular market index. An ETF is similar to an index fund in that it will primarily invest in the securities of companies that are included in a selected market index. An ETF will invest in either all of the securities or a representative sample of the securities included in the index. For example, one type of ETF, known as Spiders or SPDRs, invests in all of the stocks contained in the S&P 500 Composite Stock Price Index. ETFs are a quick and easy way for investors, with only a small amount of money to invest, to create a diversified portfolio. ETF's as the name suggests, trade on a stock exchange, such as the NYSE and can be bought or sold during the hours that the stock market is open for trading (Monday through Friday from 9:30 a.m.–4 pm). Mutual funds, on the other hand, can only be purchased after the close of the trading at a preset price (the Net Asset Value or NAV of the fund) on a given day.

Fiscal year—The twelve-month period that a company uses to maintain its financial records and report results. The fiscal year is not required to correspond with the calendar year. Many companies have fiscal years that begin on October 1st and end on September 30th, or begin on July 1st and end on June 30th. Most companies have a fiscal year that begins on January 1st, to coincide with the calendar year, but is important to remember that many companies use other starting dates.

IPO—The letters IPO stand for Initial Public Offering. An initial public offering, also known as "going public," is the sale of newly issued stock to the public. In an IPO, investors buy stock in the newly public company. The company takes in the investors' cash and uses it to expand the business or pay off earlier private investors in the business such as the company's founders and venture capitalists. Prior to the IPO, the business was a private company. Following the IPO, it is a public company with shares that trades on a public stock exchange.

Liquidity—The measure of an investor's ability to buy or sell an investment quickly, and at a price very close to the price of a similar prior transaction. For example, the markets for stocks and bonds are extremely liquid. Investors can buy or sell hundreds or thousands of shares in a matter of seconds, without affecting the price by more than a few pennies per share. Real estate, on the other hand, is relatively illiquid. It can often take weeks or months to sell a piece of property, and often at a price far different from the price that a similar parcel sold for in a recent transaction.

Market Capitalization—or market cap. is the size of a publicly traded corporation. The size is determined by the number of shares outstanding multiplied by the price per share. The total market cap is theoretically the amount of money you would need to spend to buy every share of the corporation's stock and in effect, own the entire corporation. Return to our pizza analogy, the market cap is the size of the pizza pie—it is the number of slices (shares) multiplied by the size of each slice (price per share in dollars).

NASDAQ—National Association of Securities Dealers Automated Quotations—a computerized data system to provide brokers with price quotations for securities traded "over the counter." Like the NYSE, the NASDAQ connects buyers and sellers of stocks. However, unlike the NYSE, it has no physical location and there are no specialists that maintain markets in individual stocks. Liquidity for each stock is created by brokers and dealers who maintain markets in various securities. Unlike the NYSE, where a specialist maintains a market, popular NASDAQ stocks such as Microsoft and Intel may have dozens of dealers who maintain a market in those stocks. These dealers hold inventory of a particular stock and offer to buy and sell shares at prices referred to as the bid price (the price at which they will buy stock from you, the seller) and the offer or ask price (the price at which you may buy stock from them). The difference between the bid and the ask price is referred to as, "the spread." Dealers earn profits by buying stock from the public at the lower bid price and attempting to resell it at the higher ask price. Unlike the NYSE, buyers and sellers do not physically meet in a central location.

NYSE—The New York Stock Exchange—This is the physical location where buyers and sellers meet to trade shares of stocks that are listed on the NYSE. This trading occurs on the Exchange's trading floors located at the corner of Wall and Broad Streets in lower Manhattan. Buyers and sellers are matched up by a *specialist*, who maintains a post on the floor of the Exchange. Every stock traded on the Exchange has an assigned specialist, whose function is to match up buyers and sellers and maintain an orderly and liquid market in his particular stock. This ensures that shares of stock can be bought or sold quickly, with relatively small transaction costs.

P/E Ratio—The price earnings ratio—simply the price of the stock divided by the earnings per share. To calculate the *trailing P/E ratio*, divide the stock price by the company earnings for the past twelve months. To calculate the *forward P/E ratio*, divide the stock price by the expected earnings for the coming twelve-month period (the forward p/e will always be an estimated measurement). The P/E ratio is a quick and simple method for assessing a company's valuation in determining whether the stock is cheap or expensive. It is important that investors look at other valuation measures besides the P/E ratio and understand that a low P/E does not necessarily equate to a cheap or attractive stock and the reverse is true for stocks with high P/E ratios.

Ticker Symbol—Every stock has a unique one to four letter symbol that identifies the stock as being that of a specific company. Stocks that trade on the New York Stock Exchange have one to three letter symbols. Stocks on the NASDAQ have four letter symbols. Occasionally, certain foreign stocks or stocks of companies in bankruptcy will be assigned five letter symbols. Ticker symbols can eliminate confusion when placing an order to buy or sell a particular stock. For example, Cisco, the data networking company, can easily be confused with Sysco, the food service company. However, the ticker symbol for Cisco is CSCO (its shares trade on the NASDAQ), whereas the ticker symbol for Sysco is SYY (its shares trade on the New York Stock Exchange).

978-0-595-42751-2
0-595-42751-0

Printed in the United States
81481LV00002B/550-699